Collins

need to know?

Ballroom Dancing

Lyndon Wainwright
with Lynda King

Collins

First published in 2007 by Collins
an imprint of
HarperCollins Publishers
77–85 Fulham Palace Road
London W6 8JB

www.collins.co.uk

10 09 08 07 06
6 5 4 3 2 1

Text © Lyndon Wainwright, 2005, 2006
Design, step-by-step photographs and illustrations
© HarperCollins Publishers, 2005, 2006
Photographs © Bananastock Ltd., Corbis, Getty Images, Lyndon
Wainwright (see also Acknowledgements on page 191)

A catalogue record for this book is available from the British Library

Lyndon Wainwright asserts the moral right to be identified as the
author of this work.

Created by: m&n publishing
Editor: Nina Sharman
Designer: Martin Hendry
Photographer: Christopher H. D. Davis
Illustrator: Lee Woodgate
Dance consultant: Lynda King
Series design: Mark Thomson
Cover photographs: © Bananastock Ltd.

Based on material from *Let's Dance* by Lyndon Wainwright

ISBN-13: 978-0-00-723023-5
ISBN-10: 0-00-723023-0

Colour reproduction by Colourscan, Singapore
Printed and bound by Printing Express Ltd., Hong Kong

Contents

Introduction

The instruction in this book will allow you to join in those dances the worldwide dance profession calls ballroom dancing. Learn the steps and you will be able to enjoy the fun at a public dance, on holiday, at a dinner dance, at a wedding reception and so on. Waltz, Slow Foxtrot, Tango and Quickstep are explained as they are regarded by the ballroom teaching profession as 'ballroom'. Additionally, because they are so popular and such an important part of a dancer's repertoire, two other dances are included, namely the Social Foxtrot and the Rock 'n' Roll/Jive.

Clear step-by-step instructions are given for the fundamental elements of each dance and the jargon used by experienced dancers has been avoided. The figures included are sufficient to allow you to enjoy each dance and will give you a basis on which you will be able to enlarge your repertoire.

The dances explained are all for couples and no solo dances such as those seen in discos are included. Dancing by couples has a long history and it is not unreasonable to say that they are part of your heritage. Dancing in couples as a pastime goes back certainly to the time of Elizabeth I and before.

There are many reasons why such dancing has survived and currently is attracting so much attention and interest. It is, of course, great fun to do and this is the main reason for doing it, but there are other benefits. It helps to keep you fit, it exercises your brain, and, for the young, it provides a valuable lesson in self discipline. It is a very social activity bringing people together and providing a valuable boy meets girl, indeed man meets woman, element.

If you have not danced before, the pages that follow will open up for you a social activity and grace that should give you a great deal of enjoyment and keep you physically and mentally fit.

Author Lyndon Wainwright and his dance partner Felicia (opposite) strike a pose while dancing the ballroom Tango.

1 Preparing to dance

Learning to dance is not only an excellent physical activity, it also improves posture and keeps you mentally alert. Above all, it is fantastic fun – so get ready to dance. It is music that determines the style of dance, and beginners should learn to listen for the all-important rhythm. Advice on ballroom dancing music is given here, together with information on what to wear. The main holds and positions used in ballroom dancing are explained, as well as how to use this book.

Ballroom dancing history

Dancing in various forms has existed since before 10,000 BC. Prehistoric man made drawings of men and women dancing together on the wall of a cave in Cogul, Northern Spain.

Homer in his writings (c.1,400–1,200 BC) describes circular and linear dances, albeit in a very crude form. Our forebears going back many thousands of years danced; indeed dancing is one of the most instinctive of all human activities.

Historically, dance has been used to serve many functions. There have been war dances, courtship dances, religious and voodoo dances, and in some primitive societies these still exist. Indeed many would argue that even now much of dancing is a courtship dance.

Dance forms change with the passage of time. It is an inevitable process. In the years up to 1500, examples of the popular dances are: Brawles, Farandoes and Basse; while in the period up to 1900, Pavane, Galliard, Volta, Minuet, Gavotte, Hornpipe, Waltz and Polka were danced. The 20th century heralded the modern Waltz, Slow Foxtrot, Quickstep, Tango, Rock 'n' Roll and the various Latin dances such as the Rumba.

The ballroom dances included in this book are all danced throughout the world. In the late 1920s British dance teachers felt the need to have some standardization of what they taught so that a dancer moving from one area of the country to another would find the same dances and figures being used. This led to the formation in 1929 of the so-called

did you know?

Championship titles
The most prestigious titles are the British Open for Ballroom and for Latin dancing. These two professional championships are run each year in Blackpool and attract couples from all over the world. In 2006 the professional ballroom championship attracted 309 couples while the Latin professional had 280 competitors. In the final round of the competitions there were couples from China, Denmark, England, Germany, Italy, Poland, Russia, Slovenia, and USA.

Official Board of Ballroom Dancing, later to be renamed the British Dance Council (B.D.C.).

This body standardized at that time, six dances. These were Quickstep, Waltz, Slow Foxtrot, Tango, Blues, and a new dance, the G/O. The first four are still with us. As well as standardizing basic figures in the dances, the committee also established rules for dance competitions and defined amateur and professional status for such events.

Its work survived and became endorsed to the extent that in 1950 the B.D.C. called a conference to consider all the world adopting the guidelines it had laid down. Duly, the International Council of Ballroom Dancing was established for this purpose.

Dancers in the 1950s take to the floor to enjoy a formal band. At this time the standard dance band comprised fourteen musicians: one on violin, four on rhythm, four on saxophones and five on brass.

Ballroom dance music

Music determines what particular dance you are going to perform. Each dance has its own distinctive music and you need to learn how much music is required for each step.

We are accustomed to thinking of dancing as being something performed to music, but at its most elementary any rhythmic beat will suffice. The ticking of a metronome could do as a basis for dance steps. Of course, while the metronome does give a rhythm, it lacks any variety and expression. The rhythm section of an orchestra produces a great variety of moods and expression. The melody complements the rhythms giving more depth and colour to any musical piece.

From the point of view of the beginner it is the rhythm that is all important and for which you must listen. All the dances in this book are in 4/4 or 2/4 time except for the Waltz which is in 3/4 time. In the case of 4/4 and 2/4 time you can count two slows or four quicks in a bar of music. In most such music the beats are of more even emphasis than those of the Waltz. Much pop music has very pronounced beats indeed and can often be felt through the floor as well as be heard. Generally, the first and third beat of the four are more pronounced than the second and fourth. You should be able to hear the four beats, and the pronounced beats should also be obvious.

Twin-kle, twin-kle, lit - tle star, How I won-der what you are

In the first of these four bars of music from the popular nursery rhyme, each 'twinkle' takes two musical crotchets, that is two 'quick' counts. In bar two, 'little' takes two counts, and 'star' takes one 'slow' count.

Dress to dance

When choosing what to wear, whether for practise or for social dancing, bear in mind comfort. In ballroom dancing, clothing ranges from long, flowing ballgowns to short, free-moving skirts.

While there are not as many ballrooms as once there were, there are still many places where dancing takes place, including hotels, clubs, public halls and some larger dance schools. Dress for both men and women will be dictated by the venue and the style of dance. However, whatever you wear should be comfortable and appropriate for the particular dance. Clothing should not be too restricting, especially around the legs – this is especially true for women. It is important that you are able to move the arms, legs and hips freely.

Shoes are of vital importance. They should be lightweight and with a flexible sole, if possible a leather sole. Good dancers use shoes with special 'non-skid' soles made of chrome leather or similar, but at the beginner level this is not necessary. However, the sole of the shoes should not impede movement of the foot across the floor in steps where you stroke the floor with the foot. Men should wear good-quality dress shoes.

Immaculate, formal attire is worn for ballroom dancing competitions.

Women should wear shoes with heels, but not stilettos. This will assist balance on backwards steps in ballroom, especially when the lady has more of these than the man.

Dance holds and positions

Before starting to dance you will need to learn the correct holds. Couples should stand up straight with long spines. Generally, for ballroom dancing, the Close Hold is adopted.

Close Hold

This is a body contact hold but less relaxed than the Cuddle Hold described below. Both the man and lady should stand up well, with the lady's right hip positioned roughly midway between the

The Close Hold is used for most ballroom dances.

The Cuddle Hold is used mostly in social dancing and is very relaxed.

Here, dancers demonstrate the positioning of hands used in ballroom dances such as the Social Foxtrot.

man's hips. The man holds the lady with his right hand placed well round her back. The lady rests her left hand on the man's upper right arm just below or on his shoulder. The man holds the lady's right hand in his left hand. Good dancers may hold the hands fairly high but, to start with, the man's left hand should be about level with his chin and neck. According to your relative sizes, the hold can be adjusted but the man needs to hold the lady firmly without overdoing the pressure.

Cuddle Hold

Both man and lady should stand up well, facing each other and in a relaxed position avoiding tension. The lady's right hip should contact the man roughly midway across his body. The man's right hand and arm go well round the lady so his hand rests under her right shoulder. Keep the fingers of the right hand close together and bent, not straight. The lady rests her left hand on the man's shoulder and if the mood takes her can go round the man's neck. The man holds the lady's right hand in his left with his fingers across the knuckles of the lady's hand. (Hands can be held level with his neck, with his left elbow away from the body so that the angle at the elbow is preferably less than 45 degrees.) The most important thing is you should try to feel comfortable.

Dancers' feet in promenade position, which occurs in many dances. The man's left and lady's right sides are turned away from one another allowing them both to step forwards with the man's right and the lady's left foot.

How to use this book

Popular ballroom dances are introduced with the assumption that readers are novices. The figures (or the routines) in each dance have been chosen to get you dancing as soon as possible.

Many of the dances in this book show simplified versions of more sophisticated figures in the hope that the experience and joy of dancing and moving to music will encourage you to delve more deeply. A visit to a local school of dance will broaden your horizons immensely. As with all disciplines, a jargon has grown up around dance analysis and here it is used only if it provides a useful shortcut to learning (see Glossary on page 182).

Although it is not crucial, all figures start on the man's left and the lady's right foot. This helps overcome some of the uncertainty beginners have at the start of a dance.

In each figure, foot diagrams of the steps are included as an aid to following the instructions (see opposite). While these are as accurate as possible, in some cases it has been necessary to exaggerate the size of the steps in order to avoid having too many on the same point.

With the exception of Tango, the dances described fall into two categories. The first includes the moving dances, such as the Waltz and Quickstep; the second mostly includes the dances that have developed for use when floor space is limited, for instance, the Social Foxtrot and Rock 'n' Roll. In the moving dances most forwards steps, taken by either the man or lady, are similar to walking and taken on the heel of the stepping foot.

In the non-moving dances all steps at beginner level are taken on the ball of the foot with the heel settling to the floor immediately after the foot is in position.

> **must know**
>
> **Steps and figures**
> A step is the movement of a foot from one position to its next position, while a group of steps is known as a figure. Each dance, for instance, Waltz or Quickstep, comprises several individual figures that can be joined together to form a routine. In each dance suggestions are given for ways of grouping figures.

This is the name of the figure. Dances comprise individual figures that are joined together, sometimes one after another, or in a particular grouping.

A bold solid line denotes the wall. This will help you to know where to start.

When you see a dotted foot, it means that you move your foot slightly after you have taken the main step.

On the foot diagrams, start positions for the man and the lady are given for all figures. Note that the pale foot is the left and the dark foot the right.

The length of some steps has been slightly exaggerated so that it is clear where each foot has to move to.

The Progressive Boxes

Once you have mastered the two basic turns you can amalgamate them. Dance the preparatory step and 1–6 of the Right

Box with Right Turn. Follow with steps 4–6 of the Left Box with Left Turn and then 1–3 of the Left Box with Left Turn.

must know

Musical tempo
This sequence of 12 steps will take you around the room and can be repeated as many times as you wish. Remember that the slow count is two beats of music and the quick count one beat.

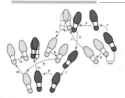

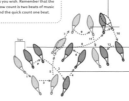

Man's Steps

count

slow	P Left foot takes a small step to the side.
slow	1 Right foot takes a step forwards, turning to the right.
quick	2 Left foot takes a step to the side, still turning to the right.
quick	3 Right foot closes to left foot, still turning to the right.
slow	4 Left foot takes a step backwards, still turning to the right.
quick	5 Right foot takes a step to the side, still turning to the right.
quick	6 Left foot closes to right foot, completing the right turn
slow	7 Right foot takes a step backwards, turning to the left.
quick	8 Left foot takes a step to the side, still turning to the left.
quick	9 Right foot closes to left foot, still turning to the left. c
slow	10 Left foot takes a step forwards, still turning to the left.
quick	11 Right foot takes a step to the side, still turning to the left.
quick	12 Left foot closes to right foot, completing the left turn.

Lady's Steps

count

slow	P Right foot takes a small step to the side.
slow	1 Left foot takes a step backwards, turning to the right.
quick	2 Right foot takes a step to the side, still turning to the right.
quick	3 Left foot closes to right foot, still turning to the right.
slow	4 Right foot takes a step forwards, still turning to the right.
quick	5 Left foot takes a step to the side, still turning to the right.
quick	6 Right foot closes to left foot, completing the right turn.
slow	7 Left foot takes a step forwards, turning to the left.
quick	8 Right foot takes a step to the side, still turning to the left.
quick	9 Left foot closes to right foot, still turning to the left.
slow	10 Right foot takes a step backwards, still turning to the left.
quick	11 Left foot takes a step to the side, still turning to the left.
quick	12 Right foot closes to left foot, completing the left turn.

If you learn the musical count, it will help you to maintain a good rhythm when dancing.

By reading the step-by-step instructions in conjunction with the diagrams, you will be able to practise the movements of each figure without a partner.

The Link

1
count: quick

M Left foot takes a small step backwards.

L Right foot takes a small step backwards.

2
count: quick

M Right foot remains in place and weight is taken firmly forwards onto it.

L Left foot remains in place and weight is taken firmly forwards onto it.

3
count: slow

M Left foot takes a small step forwards, drawing the lady towards you to regain normal hold.

L Right foot takes a small step forwards, to regain normal hold.

4
count: slow

M Right foot takes a small step to the side in normal hold.

L Left foot takes a small step to the side in normal hold.

The step-by-step photographs generally show the position you and your partner will be in at the end of each instruction.

The man's and lady's instructions here are slightly abridged versions of those that accompany the foot diagrams. They read from left to right.

2 Social Foxtrot

Not to be confused with the much more
difficult Slow Foxtrot, the Social Foxtrot
is the first dance in this book for several
reasons. Primarily it is here because you
will quickly learn enough steps to enable
you to join in the dancing. The rhythms and
the steps of the figures employed are simple
and, because the steps in the figures are
fairly small, the Social Foxtrot can be danced
on modest and very crowded floors. This
dance has been around since the early
20th century and can be danced to music in
common time, which is that used in most
popular music, and at a wide range of speeds.

A popular dance

The Social Foxtrot is found on dance floors around the world. However, when it emerged in the early 1900s and flourished in the jazz era, it was considered to be a rebellious dance style.

The Foxtrot is named after an American actor, Harry Fox, whose real name was Arthur Carringford; he called himself Fox after his grandfather. As part of his vaudeville act Harry Fox performed a comic walk, accompanied by ragtime music, which became known as 'Fox's Trot'. In April 1914, Harry was presenting his act as part of a theatrical interlude in between films at Hammerstein's – a movie house that had been converted from one of the largest theatres in the world. There was a roof garden above the theatre, called the 'Jardin de Danse', and the management wanted to promote Harry and exploit his 'Fox's Trot', so they included it in the dance repertoire for the general public in the roof garden. The name has lived on as Foxtrot, although there are variations of the name.

Music and the dance

This is the most universally popular dance for couples. It can be danced to any music in 4/4 (common) time and the speed of the music is not a determining factor. The Social Foxtrot is a dance in which partners keep close contact with each other and do not move a great deal and is known by many names such as 'crush dancing', 'Rhythm dancing', 'café style', 'American Foxtrot'. These names tell you a great deal about the dance. Any time you see the general public dancing in a film and the music is in common time this is the dance most of the couples will be doing.

must know

Positive leading
It is important for the man to hold the lady firmly in order to guide her through the steps. Social Foxtrot is not a 'moving dance'. In most moving dances the flow of the dance is a significant aid to guiding your partner; because it does not exist in Social Foxtrot the lead needs to be especially positive.

As you will see in the Left Box (see pages 22-3), some steps take two beats and some one. Any mental count that helps you remember the steps and keep in time with the music is acceptable.

In the Social Foxtrot use the Cuddle Hold as here, always remembering to maintain body contact.

The hold and leading

In this dance you use the Cuddle Hold (see page 14-15). The man leads or guides the lady through the figures and, as the name implies, you do not take long steps in this dance. It is important that you maintain the body contact because this is where the lead originates. The man can help by holding the lady close to him with his right hand, but don't forget that she does need to breathe. The lady needs to try to keep relaxed and not to fight against the lead that comes from the man. If the mood takes the lady and she wants to nestle her head on her partner's shoulder and snuggle up to him, well, why not?

The Left Box

Learn the following steps solo but as soon as possible try them with a partner. Do not try to stride out too much. Steps taken forwards and backwards should be just be a little shorter than normal walking steps and side steps about, say, two shoe widths. When you have a partner, place your hands on his or her shoulders so that you can see how the steps follow each other.

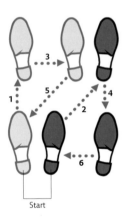

Start

Man's Steps

count:

Start by facing the nearest wall. Take the weight onto your right foot so that, while your left foot remains in contact with the floor, it is free to move without having to make any weight change.

slow **1** **Left foot** takes a step forwards, taking two beats of music.

quick **2** **Right foot** takes a step to the side on the same line as left foot, taking one beat of music.

quick **3** **Left foot** closes to right foot, transferring weight onto left foot, and taking one beat of music.

slow **4** **Right foot** takes a step backwards, taking two beats of music.

quick **5** **Left foot** takes a step to the side on the same line as right foot, taking one beat of music.

quick **6** **Right foot** closes to left foot, transferring weight onto right foot and taking one beat of music.

must know

Hold and lead
As soon as both of you are confident with the step pattern, stand close to one another with bodies touching at the hips. The man should hold the lady firmly so that she can feel him placing the weight onto his right foot and that should indicate to her to settle her weight onto her left foot.

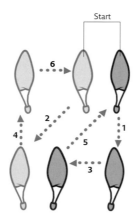

Start

Lady's Steps

counts

Start with your back to the nearest wall. Take the weight onto your left foot so that, while your right foot remains in contact with the floor, it is free to move without having to make any weight change.

slow 1 Right foot takes a step backwards, taking two beats of music.

quick 2 Left foot takes a step to the side, on the same line as right foot, taking one beat of music.

quick 3 Right foot closes to left foot, transferring weight onto right foot and taking one beat of music.

slow 4 Left foot takes a step forwards, taking two beats of music.

quick 5 Right foot takes a step to the side on the same line as left foot, taking one beat of music.

quick 6 Left foot closes to right foot, transferring weight onto left foot and taking one beat of music.

The Left Box with Left Turn

Once you are happy that you have mastered the foot pattern of the Left Box (see pages 22–3) then you can start to add turns to the figure.

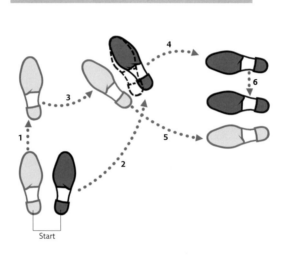

Start

count: **Man's Steps**

Start by facing the nearest wall, and on all steps turn a little to your left.

slow 1 Left foot takes a step forwards, turning to the left, that is, bringing the right side of your body forwards as you step and taking two beats of music.

quick 2 Right foot takes a step to the side, still turning to the left and taking one beat of music.

quick 3 Left foot closes to right foot, still turning to the left and taking one beat of music.

slow 4 Right foot takes a step backwards, still turning to the left, that is, bringing the left side of your body backwards and taking two beats of music.

quick 5 Left foot takes a step to the side, still turning to the left and taking one beat of music.

quick 6 Right foot closes to left foot, still turning to the left and taking one beat of music.

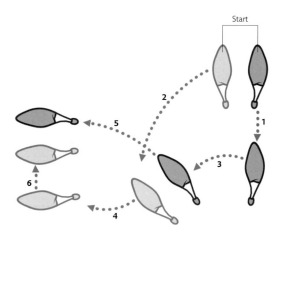

count: ## Lady's Steps

Start with your back to the nearest wall, and on all steps turn a little to your left.

slow 1 Right foot takes a step backwards, turning to the left and taking two beats of music.

quick 2 Left foot takes a step to the side, still turning to the left and taking one beat of music.

quick 3 Right foot closes to left foot, still turning to the left and taking one beat of music.

slow 4 Left foot takes a step forwards, still turning to the left and taking two beats of music.

quick 5 Right foot takes a step to the side, still turning to the left and taking one beat of music.

quick 6 Left foot closes to right foot, still turning to the left and taking one beat of music.

The Left Box

1

count: slow

M Left foot takes a step forwards.

L Right foot takes a step backwards.

Takes two beats of music.

2

count: quick

M Right foot takes a step to the side on the same line as left foot.

L Left foot takes a step to the side, on the same line as right foot.

Takes one beat of music.

4

count: slow

M Right foot takes a step backwards.

L Left foot takes a step forwards.

Takes two beats of music.

5

count: quick

M Left foot takes a step to the side on the same line as right foot.

L Right foot takes a step to the side on the same line as left foot.

Takes one beat of music.

3

count: quick

M **Left foot** closes
to right foot,
transferring
weight onto foot.

L **Right foot** closes
to left foot,
transferring
weight onto foot.

Takes one beat
of music.

6

count: quick

M **Right foot** closes
to left foot,
transferring
weight onto foot.

L **Left foot** closes
to right foot,
transferring
weight onto foot.

Takes one beat
of music.

must know

Close contact
Remember that the Social
Foxtrot is a dance in which
partners keep close
contact with each other
and do not move a great
deal. It is a dance that
beginners can master
and enjoy

The Right Box

In this figure, a preparatory side step (weight change step) has been introduced so that both the man and the lady always start on the same foot. Steps 1–6 (inclusive) of the Right Box can be repeated.

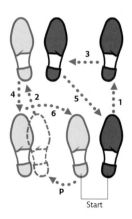

Start

Man's Steps

count:

Start by standing erect, in close body contact with your partner and facing the nearest wall. As a result of the preparatory step to your left side, you will be free to move off with your right foot into the Right Box itself.

slow **P** **Left foot** takes a small step to the side, taking two beats of music.

slow **1** **Right foot** takes a step forwards, taking two beats of music.

quick **2** **Left foot** takes a step to the side onto the same line as right foot, taking one beat of music.

quick **3** **Right foot** closes to left foot, transferring weight onto right foot and taking one beat of music.

slow **4** **Left foot** takes a step backwards, taking two beats of music.

quick **5** **Right foot** takes a step to the side onto the same line as left foot, taking one beat of music.

quick **6** **Left foot** closes to right foot, transferring weight onto left foot and taking one beat of music.

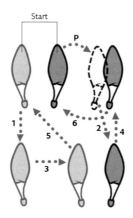

Lady's Steps

Start by standing erect, in close body contact with your partner and backing the nearest wall. As a result of the preparatory step to your right side, you will be free to move off with your left foot when you feel the man move off with his right foot.

slow **P** **Right foot** takes a small step to the side, taking two beats of music.

slow **1** **Left foot** takes a step backwards, taking two beats of music.

quick **2** **Right foot** takes a step to the side on the same line as left foot, taking one beat of music.

quick **3** **Left foot** closes to right foot, transferring weight onto left foot and taking one beat of music.

slow **4** **Right foot** takes a step forwards, taking two beats of music.

quick **5** **Left foot** takes a step to the side onto the same line as right foot, taking one beat of music.

quick **6** **Right foot** closes to left foot, transferring weight onto right foot and taking one beat of music.

The Right Box

P
count: slow

M **Left foot** takes a small step to the side.

L **Right foot** takes a small step to the side.

Takes two beats of music.

1
count: slow

M **Right foot** takes a step forwards.

L **Left foot** takes a step backwards.

Takes two beats of music.

4
count: slow

M **Left foot** takes a step backwards.

L **Right foot** takes a step forwards.

Takes two beats of music.

2

count: quick

M **Left foot** takes a step to the side on the same line as right foot.

L **Right foot** takes a step to the side on the same line as left foot.

Takes one beat of music.

3

count: quick

M **Right foot** closes to left foot, transferring weight onto right foot.

L **Left foot** closes to right foot, transferring weight onto left foot.

Takes one beat of music.

5

count: quick

M **Right foot** takes a step to the side, on the same line as left foot.

L **Left foot** takes a step to the side, on the same line as left foot.

Takes one beat of music.

6

count: quick

M **Left foot** closes to right foot, transferring weight onto left foot.

L **Right foot** closes to left foot, transferring weight onto right foot.

Takes one beat of music.

The Right Box with Right Turn

The Right Box with Right Turn comprises steps 1–6 omitting the preparatory step.

As with the Right Box, Steps 1–6 (inclusive) can be repeated.

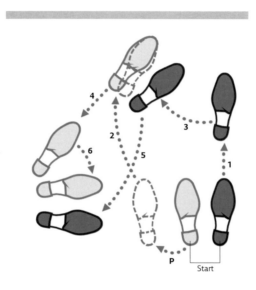

count: **Man's Steps**

Start by facing the nearest wall.

slow **P** Left foot takes a small step to the side, taking two beats of music.

slow **1** Right foot takes a step forwards, turning to the right, that is, bringing the left side of your body forwards as you step and taking two beats of music.

quick **2** Left foot takes a step to the side, still turning to the right and taking one beat of music.

quick **3** Right foot closes to left foot, still turning to the right and taking one beat of music.

slow **4** Left foot takes a step backwards, still turning to the right, that is, bringing the right side of your body backwards and taking two beats of music.

quick **5** Right foot takes a step to the side, still turning to the right and taking one beat of music.

quick **6** Left foot closes to right foot, still turning to the right and taking one beat of music.

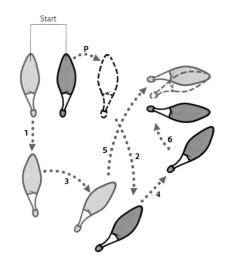

count:	**Lady's Steps**

Start with your back to the nearest wall.

slow P Right foot takes a small step to the side, taking two beats of music.

slow 1 Left foot takes a step backwards, turning to the right and taking two beats of music.

quick 2 Right foot takes a step to the side, still turning to the right and taking one beat of music.

quick 3 Left foot closes to right foot, still turning to the right and taking one beat of music.

slow 4 Right foot takes a step forwards, still turning to the right and taking two beats of music.

quick 5 Left foot takes a step to the side, still turning to the right, taking one beat of music.

quick 6 Right foot closes to left foot, still turning to the right and taking one beat of music.

The Right Box with Right Turn

P

count: slow

M Left foot takes
a small step to
the side.

L Right foot takes
a small step to
the side.

Takes two beats
of music.

1

count: slow

M Right foot takes
a step forwards,
turning to
the right.

L Left foot takes a
step backwards,
turning to
the right.

Takes two beats
of music.

4

count: slow

M Left foot takes a
step backwards,
still turning to
the right.

L Right foot takes
a step forwards,
still turning to
the right.

Takes two beats
of music.

2

count: quick

M Left foot takes a
step to the side,
still turning to
the right.

L Right foot takes
a step to the side,
still turning to
the right.

Takes one beat
of music.

3

count: quick

M Right foot closes
to left foot,
still turning to
the right.

L Left foot closes
to right foot,
still turning to
the right.

Takes one beat
of music.

5

count: quick

M Right foot takes
a step to the side,
still turning to
the right.

L Left foot takes a
step to the side,
still turning to
the right.

Takes one beat
of music.

6

count: quick

M Left foot closes
to right foot,
still turning to
the right.

L Right foot closes
to left foot,
still turning to
the right.

Takes one beat
of music.

The Right Pivot Box

So far you have learnt the basic boxes both with and without turn. A useful and pleasant variation on the Right Box is the Right Pivot Box. The man starts by facing (and the lady by backing) diagonally to the wall (see the Glossary on page 182). Precede this figure with the first three steps of the Left Box (see pages 22-3).

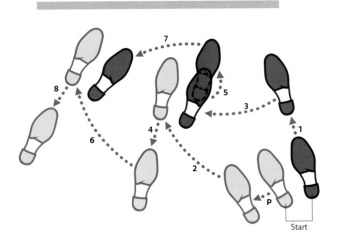

count: **Man's Steps**

Start by 'facing diagonally to wall'.

slow **P** Left foot takes a small step to the side.

slow **1** Right foot takes a step forwards, turning to the right.

quick **2** Left foot takes a step to the side, still turning to the right.

quick **3** Right foot closes to left foot, still turning to the right.

slow **4** Left foot takes a step backwards, still turning to the right and checking backwards impetus.

slow **5** Right foot takes a step slightly forwards, still turning to the right.

quick **6** Left foot takes a step to the side, still turning to the right.

quick **7** Right foot closes to left foot, still turning to the right.

slow **8** Left foot takes a step backwards, still turning to the right and checking backwards impetus.

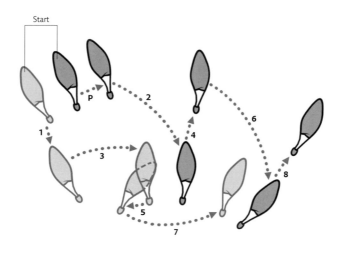

count: ## Lady's Steps

Start by 'backing diagonally to wall'.

slow **P** **Right foot** takes a small step to the side.

slow **1** **Left foot** takes a step backwards, turning to the right.

quick **2** **Right foot** takes a step to the side, still turning to the right.

quick **3** **Left foot** closes to right foot, still turning to the right.

slow **4** **Right foot** takes a step forwards, still turning to the right and responding to the man and checking his backwards impetus.

slow **5** **Left foot** takes a step slightly backwards, still turning to the right.

quick **6** **Right foot** takes a step to the side, still turning to the right.

quick **7** **Left foot** closes to right foot, still turning to the right.

slow **8** **Right foot** takes a step forwards, still turning to the right and responding to the man and checking his backwards impetus.

The Right Pivot Box

P

count: slow

M Left foot takes a small step to the side.

L Right foot takes a small step to the side.

1

count: slow

M Right foot takes a step forwards, turning to the right.

L Left foot takes a step backwards, turning to the right.

5

count: slow

M Right foot takes a step slightly forwards, turning to the right.

L Left foot takes a step slightly backwards, turning to the right.

6

count: quick

M Left foot takes a step to the side, turning to the right.

L Right foot takes a step to the side, turning to the right.

2

count: quick

M Left foot takes a step to the side, turning to the right.

L Right foot takes a step to the side, turning to the right.

3

count: quick

M Right foot closes to left foot, turning to the right.

L Left foot closes to right foot, turning to the right.

4

count: slow

M Left foot takes a step backwards, turning to the right and checking backwards impetus.

L Right foot takes a step forwards, turning to the right.

7

count: quick

M Right foot closes to left foot, turning to the right.

L Left foot closes to right foot, turning to the right.

8

count: slow

M Left foot takes a step backwards turning to the right and checking backwards impetus.

L Right foot takes a step forwards turning to the right.

The Conversation Piece

This figure is preceded by the preparatory step and steps 1–4 of the Right Box with Right Turn (see pages 32–5). You can repeat steps 3–6 of the Conversation Piece as often as you wish before going into step 7. Once you have danced the Conversation Piece, follow it with either the Left Box or steps 4–6 of the Right Box.

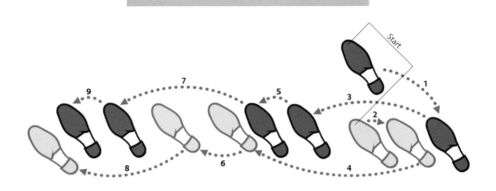

count: | **Man's Steps**

quick 1 Right foot takes a step to the side, increasing pressure on heel of right hand so that partner turns her right side away from your left side.

quick 2 Left foot closes to right foot, still turning partner so that her right side is roughly 30 cm (11¾ in) away from your left side (in promenade position).

slow 3 Right foot takes a step forwards and across left foot, partner is also stepping forwards through the space between her right and your left hips in promenade position.

quick 4 Left foot takes a step to the side and slightly forwards, still in promenade position.

quick 5 Right foot closes to left foot, still in promenade position.

slow 6 Left foot takes a step to the side and slightly forwards, still in promenade position.

slow 7 Right foot takes a step forwards and across the left foot, still in promenade position.

quick 8 Left foot takes a step to the side, commencing to guide the lady to face you again.

quick 9 Right foot closes to left foot, keeping pressure on tips of right fingers to guide the lady into normal hold.

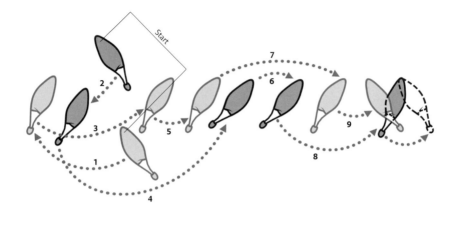

Lady's Steps

count:

quick 1 Left foot takes a step to the side, turning to the right so that your right side turns away from the man's left side.

quick 2 Right foot closes to left foot, still turning so that your right side is roughly 30 cm (11¾ in) away from the man's left side (in promenade position).

slow 3 Left foot takes a step forwards and across right foot, partner is also stepping forwards through the space between your right and his left hips in promenade position.

quick 4 Right foot takes a step to the side and slightly forwards still in promenade position.

quick 5 Left foot closes to right foot, still in promenade position.

slow 6 Right foot takes a step to the side and slightly forwards, still in promenade position.

slow 7 Left foot takes a step forwards and across the right foot still in promenade position.

quick 8 Right foot takes a step to the side, but starting to turn to face the man again.

quick 9 Left foot closes to right foot, completing turn towards the man to regain normal hold.

The Conversation Piece

1
count: quick

M **Right foot** takes a step to the side, guiding partner to turn right.

L **Left foot** takes a step to the side, turning to the right away from the man's left side.

2
count: quick

M **Left foot** closes to right foot, still turning partner to the right.

L **Right foot** closes to left foot, still turning to the right into promenade position.

3
count: slow

M **Right foot** forwards and across your left foot.

L **Left foot** forwards and across your right foot.

Both man and lady in promenade position.

6
count: slow

M **Left foot** to the side and slightly forwards.

L **Right foot** to the side and slightly forwards.

Both man and lady in promenade position.

7
count: slow

M **Right foot** forwards and across left foot.

L **Left foot** forwards and across right foot.

Both man and lady in promenade position.

4

count: quick

M Left foot to the side and slightly forwards.

L Right foot to the side and slightly forwards.

Both man and lady in promenade position.

5

count: quick

M Right foot closes to left foot.

L Left foot closes to right foot.

Both man and lady in promenade position.

8

count: quick

M Left foot to the side, guiding the lady to face you again.

L Right foot to the side, turning to face the man again.

9

count: quick

M Right foot closes to left foot, guiding partner into normal hold.

L Left foot closes to right foot, completing turn towards the man to regain normal hold.

The Progressive Boxes

Once you have mastered the two basic turns you can amalgamate them. Dance the preparatory step and 1–6 of the Right Box with Right Turn. Follow with steps 4–6 of the Left Box with Left Turn and then 1–3 of the Left Box with Left Turn.

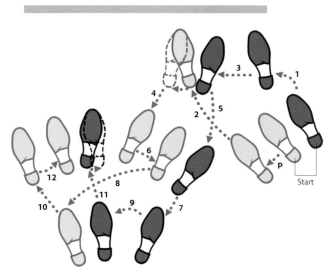

Man's Steps

Start by 'facing diagonally to wall'.

count:		
slow	**P**	**Left foot** takes a small step to the side.
slow	**1**	**Right foot** takes a step forwards, turning to the right.
quick	**2**	**Left foot** takes a step to the side, still turning to the right.
quick	**3**	**Right foot** closes to left foot, still turning to the right.
slow	**4**	**Left foot** takes a step backwards, still turning to the right.
quick	**5**	**Right foot** takes a step to the side, still turning to the right.
quick	**6**	**Left foot** closes to right foot, completing the right turn.
slow	**7**	**Right foot** takes a step backwards, turning to the left.
quick	**8**	**Left foot** takes a step to the side, still turning to the left.
quick	**9**	**Right foot** closes to left foot, still turning to the left.
slow	**10**	**Left foot** takes a step forwards, still turning to the left.
quick	**11**	**Right foot** takes a step to the side, still turning to the left.
quick	**12**	**Left foot** closes to right foot, completing the left turn.

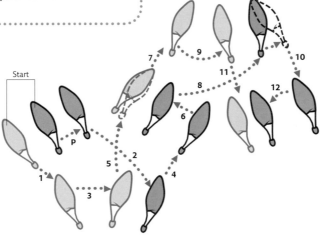

count:

Lady's Steps

Start by 'backing diagonally to wall'.

count		
slow	**P**	**Right foot** takes a small step to the side.
slow	**1**	**Left foot** takes a step backwards, turning to the right.
quick	**2**	**Right foot** takes a step to the side, still turning to the right.
quick	**3**	**Left foot** closes to right foot, still turning to the right.
slow	**4**	**Right foot** takes a step forwards, still turning to the right.
quick	**5**	**Left foot** takes a step to the side, still turning to the right.

count		
quick	**6**	**Right foot** closes to left foot, completing the right turn.
slow	**7**	**Left foot** takes a step forwards, turning to the left.
quick	**8**	**Right foot** takes a step to the side, still turning to the left.
quick	**9**	**Left foot** closes to right foot, still turning to the left.
slow	**10**	**Right foot** takes a step backwards, still turning to the left.
quick	**11**	**Left foot** takes a step to the side, still turning to the left.
quick	**12**	**Right foot** closes to left foot, completing the left turn.

The Progressive Boxes

P

count: slow

M Left foot takes a small step to the side.

L Right foot takes a small step to the side.

1

count: slow

M Right foot takes a step forwards, turning to the right.

L Left foot takes a step backwards, turning to the right.

must know

Turning technique

In the Progressive Boxes the man turns to the right on the first six steps and to the left on the next six. The turns should be roughly equal so that at the end of the sequence the man is facing in the same direction as that in which he started (even though the couple have moved around the room). After step 12, the man steps forwards with his right foot to start the Progressive Boxes once again.

4

count: slow

M Left foot takes a step backwards, turning to the right.

L Right foot takes a step forwards, turning to the right.

2

count: quick

M Left foot takes a step to the side, turning to the right.

L Right foot takes a step to the side, turning to the right.

3

count: quick

M Right foot closes to left foot, turning to the right.

L Left foot closes to right foot, turning to the right.

5

count: quick

M Right foot takes a step to the side, turning to the right.

L Left foot takes a step to the side, turning to the right.

6

count: quick

M Left foot closes to right foot, completing the right turn.

L Right foot closes to left foot, completing the right turn.

(continued overleaf)

The Progressive Boxes (continued)

7

count: slow

M **Right foot** takes a step backwards, turning to the left.

L **Left foot** takes a step forwards, turning to the left.

8

count: quick

M **Left foot** takes a step to the side, turning to the left.

L **Right foot** takes a step to the side, turning to the left.

10

count: slow

M **Left foot** takes a step forwards. turning to the left.

L **Right foot** takes a step backwards, turning to the left.

11

count: quick

M **Right foot** takes a step to the side, turning to the left.

L **Left foot** takes a step to the side, turning to the left.

9

count: quick

M Right foot closes
to left foot,
turning to
the left.

L Left foot closes
to right foot,
turning to
the left.

12

count: quick

M Left foot closes
to right foot,
completing the
left turn.

L Right foot closes
to left foot,
completing the
left turn.

want to know more?

• Try the Waltz next, see
pages 50–77.
• Try dancing the figures
with different partners.
• Practise dancing the
figures in rooms of any
size or shape.
• Join a dance school.
For addresses, look in
local newspapers, *Yellow
Pages*, and see Dance
studios on pages 184–9.
• Check with your local
authority for evening
classes.
• Watch the film *Mad Hot
Ballroom* – a documentary
about poor kids in New
York who learn to dance.

weblinks

• For dance history,
videos and DVDs, visit
www.centralhome.
com/ballroomcountry
/foxtrot.htm
• Learn to dance Foxtrot
in your area: www.learnto
dance.co.uk/foxtrot.htm
• See pages 183–4 for
websites of dance
teachers' organizations.

3 Waltz

Musically and as a dance the Waltz is a survivor.
It gained popularity in the earliest years of the
19th century and in one form or another has
remained an integral part of the social dance
scene ever since. Today it exists in three forms:
a fast version, the Viennese Waltz; a slower
form, the Old Time Waltz; and an even slower
version, which is seen in ballroom dancing
competitions. The latter is the version featured
here, which can also be danced at social
functions. The music has a distinct lilt and
dancers respond by rising onto the toes at
the end of each bar of music, and smoothly
lowering their heels to start the next bar. It
is delightful to experience and to watch.

A gliding dance

The Waltz has probably been around the longest out of any other current dance. It may not be the most popular, but it has seen off many dances that were temporarily more so.

The Waltz has a long history in Europe and has been taken up all over the world. It developed from peasant dances of the 16th and 17th centuries. Many authorities regard the Ländler and then the Weller as the roots of the modern dance in 3/4 time, that is, three beats to the bar of music. Both dances were popular in Austria and southern Germany, and danced to music in 3/4 time. Moreover, they were dances in which couples turned a great deal.

Types of waltz

When we now speak of waltzes we are talking about several versions. One, the so-called Viennese Waltz, is danced to fast music at a tempo of just under 60 bars per minute and is simple in its construction but more difficult in execution. To see a dance floor full of people flowing around the room dancing the Viennese Waltz is a wonderful, heady sight. Another version danced at a tempo of a little over 40 bars per minute is the Old Time Waltz. This dance, based on the five foot positions of ballet, was the popular Waltz in Britain up to World War I. It is still danced in Old Time Dance Clubs and forms the basis of many sequence dances.

At the end of the 19th and beginning of the 20th centuries an American version of waltzing, called the Boston, was popular with the dancing public. In this

did you know?

The Volta
Waltzes are danced in Close Hold, which was first seen in England in a dance called the Volta. Queen Elizabeth I was an excellent dancer and there is a famous painting at Penshurst Palace in Kent said to be of her dancing the Volta.

Waltzing couples at the Opera Ball in Vienna, Austria. This event takes places annually.

The Waltz is a gliding dance and ideally performed on modern, maple (or similar) dance floors.

the couple stood facing in opposite directions but hip to hip. Originally it was taken at about 36–38 bars per minute, but then succumbed to being a slow dance. In the current version the music tempo has dropped to 30 bars per minute and this is the one you will see in ballroom dancing competitions. In Britain, the popularity of this slow Waltz was first established in the mid-1920s when a particular version, called the Diagonal Waltz, proved successful in the World's Ballroom Dancing Championships.

Enduring quality

For evidence of the permanence of the Waltz, look at the change in the dances used in the World's Ballroom Dancing Championships over the years. The first Championships after World War I in 1919 comprised the Waltz, the Tango, the Maxixe, the One-Step and the Foxtrot. In the following year the Spanish Schottische and the Shimmy were added to the above five dances.

The Waltz and the Tango are the only dances still with us. Today's Slow Foxtrot is not the same dance as the Foxtrot of the championships at that time. It was more related to our modern Quickstep.

Modern development

One other aspect of the development of our social dances relates to the improvements in footwear and the quality of our floors. In earlier days, when modern light footwear was not available and dance floors were crude and uneven by comparison with modern maple or other dance floors, it is unlikely that the modern gliding dances could have developed.

An art form

As in all aspects of life, change is inevitable and competition drives this on. Anyone who has seen ballroom dancing at the highest level will realize that the range of advanced figures used are not those likely to be used in social dancing. An art form has grown up that is as attractive to watch as any other form of dance. Many who start dancing purely socially will find themselves caught by the bug and progress to higher or more sophisticated levels.

However, this book is an introduction to dance, aimed at inexperienced dancers. The main objective is to encourage you to get onto the dance floor so that you too can enjoy social dancing. If you decide to join a school of dance then so much the better.

Basic waltz figures

This dance is one of the so-called 'moving' dances and adopts the Close Hold throughout, maintaining body contact (see pages 14–15). The steps are fairly long compared with those of non-moving dances such as the Jive. All steps forwards should be rather like walking but the foot should skim the floor when moving to position. It is a good idea to think that the foot is caressing the floor. Sideways steps will be taken on the ball of the foot or the toes. When stepping backwards you should try to straighten the ankle so that anyone standing behind you will see the sole of your shoe. As the weight of the body moves back onto the foot this rear foot acts like a spring to help control the weight changes and the balance.

The dance is in 3/4 time and this means three beats to the bar of music. On most simple figures you will take a step on each beat in the bar.

> **did you know?**
>
> **Lord Byron**
> When the Waltz was first danced in Britain, the poet Lord Byron thought that it was immoral and wrote of it as looking like 'two cockchafers spitted on the same Bodekin'. Times have moved on!

Left and Right Changes

In this group, also known as Change Steps, the side steps (following movements forwards) will, as a result of the body flow, be slightly forwards of the line set by the supporting foot and, similarly, side steps (following movements backwards) will be slightly backwards of the line.

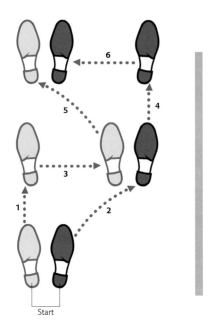

Start

Man's Steps

count:

Start with your right shoulder pointing to the nearest wall. You will be facing down the room in the direction dancers call 'facing line of dance'.

one **1** **Left foot** takes a step forwards.

two **2** **Right foot** takes a step to the side on the same line as left foot.

three **3** **Left foot** closes to right foot, taking care to place weight onto left foot (beginners sometimes don't do so).

one **4** **Right foot** takes a step forwards.

two **5** **Left foot** takes a step to the side on the same line as right foot.

three **6** **Right foot** closes to left foot taking care to place weight onto right foot (beginners sometimes don't do so).

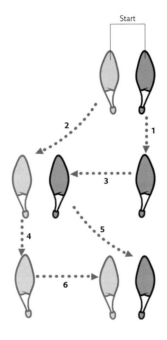

Lady's Steps

count:

Start with your left shoulder pointing to the nearest wall. You will be backing down the room in the direction dancers call 'backing line of dance'.

one **1** Right foot takes a step backwards.

two **2** Left foot takes a step to the side on the same line as right foot.

three **3** Right foot closes to left foot taking care to place weight onto right foot (beginners sometimes don't do so).

one **4** Left foot takes a step backwards.

two **5** Right foot takes a step to the side on the same line as left foot.

three **6** Left foot closes to right foot taking care to place weight onto left foot (beginners sometimes don't do so).

Left and Right Changes

1
count: one

M **Left foot** takes a step forwards.

L **Right foot** takes a step backwards.

2
count: two

M **Right foot** takes a step to the side on the same line as left foot.

L **Left foot** takes a step to the side on the same line as right foot.

4
count: one

M **Right foot** takes a step forwards.

L **Left foot** takes a step backwards.

5
count: two

M **Left foot** takes a step to the side on the same line as right foot.

L **Right foot** takes a step to the side on the same line as left foot.

3
count: three

M Left foot closes to right foot, taking weight onto left foot.

L Right foot closes to left foot, taking weight onto right foot.

6
count: three

M Right foot closes to left foot, taking weight onto right foot.

L Left foot closes to right foot, taking weight onto left foot.

must know

Taking steps
Forwards and backwards steps are walking type steps. When moving forwards they are taken on the heel. All side and closing steps should be taken on the ball of the foot or the toes. In the Waltz each step takes one beat of music, unless specified otherwise.

Left or Reverse Turn

When you feel comfortable with the Left and Right Changes (see pages 56–9), add a little variety by introducing the Left or Reverse Turn.

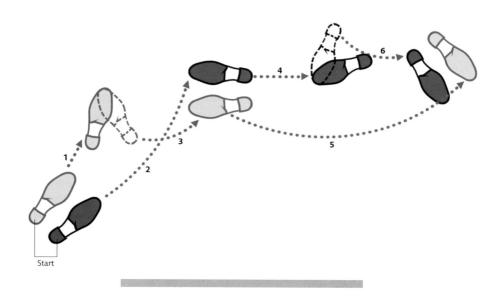

Start

Man's Steps

count:

Stand with right shoulder pointing to the nearest wall and turn about 45 degrees to the left so that you are facing slanting into the room. This commencing position is called 'facing diagonally to centre'.

one **1 Left foot** takes a step forwards, beginning to turn to left.

two **2 Right foot** takes a step to the side, still turning to the left.

three **3 Left foot** closes to right foot, still turning to left, the left shoulder should now be pointing towards the nearest wall.

one **4 Right foot** takes a step backwards, still turning to the left.

two **5 Left foot** takes a step to the side, still turning to the left.

three **6 Right foot** closes to left foot, completing the turn to the left, you should now be 'facing diagonally to wall'. Over the entire figure you should have made three-quarters of a full turn – for the mathematically inclined, 270 degrees.

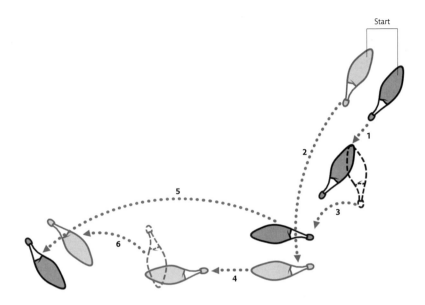

Lady's Steps

count:

Stand with left shoulder pointing to the nearest wall and slightly turn to the left so that you are facing the wall in a slanting position. This commencing position is called 'backing diagonally to centre'.

one **1** Right foot takes a step backwards, beginning to turn to left.

two **2** Left foot takes a step to the side, still turning to the left.

three **3** Right foot closes to left foot, still turning to left, the right shoulder should be pointing towards the nearest wall.

one **4** Left foot takes a step forwards, still turning to the left.

two **5** Right foot takes a step to the side, still turning to the left.

three **6** Left foot closes to right foot, completing the turn to the left, you should now be 'backing diagonally to wall'. Over the entire figure you should have made three-quarters of a full turn – for the mathematically inclined, 270 degrees.

Left or Reverse Turn

1

count: one

M Left foot takes a step forwards, beginning to turn to the left.

L Right foot takes a step backwards, beginning to turn to the left.

2

count: two

M Right foot takes a step to the side, still turning to the left.

L Left foot takes a step to the side, still turning to the left.

3

count: three

M Left foot closes to right foot, still turning to the left.

L Right foot closes to left foot, still turning to the left.

4

count: one

M Right foot takes a step backwards, still turning to the left.

L Left foot takes a step forwards, still turning to the left.

5

count: two

M Left foot takes a step to the side, still turning to the left.

L Right foot takes a step to the side, still turning to the left.

6

count: three

M Right foot closes to left foot, completing the turn to the left.

L Left foot closes to right foot, completing the turn to the left.

Right or Natural Turn

This figure is preceded and followed by Left and Right Changes. It can also follow the Reverse Turn and that amalgamation of 18 steps can be repeated.

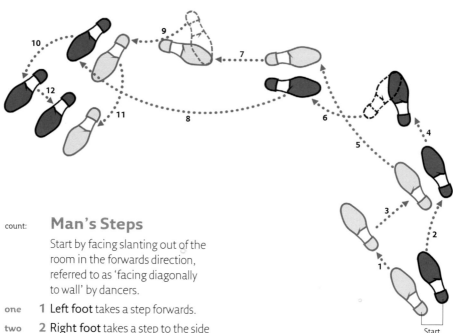

count:

Man's Steps

Start by facing slanting out of the room in the forwards direction, referred to as 'facing diagonally to wall' by dancers.

one   **1** Left foot takes a step forwards.

two   **2** Right foot takes a step to the side on the same line as the left foot.

three   **3** Left foot closes to right foot.

one   **4** Right foot takes a step forwards, beginning to turn to the right.

two   **5** Left foot takes a step to the side, still turning to the right.

three   **6** Right foot closes to left foot still turning to the right. Your left shoulder should now be pointing towards the nearest wall.

one   **7** Left foot takes a step backwards, still turning to the right.

two   **8** Right foot takes a step to the side, still turning to the right.

three   **9** Left foot closes to right foot, completing the turn to the right. You should now be 'facing diagonally to centre'.

one   **10** Right foot takes a step forwards.

two   **11** Left foot takes a step to the side on the same line as right foot.

three   **12** Right foot closes to left foot, 'facing diagonally to centre'.

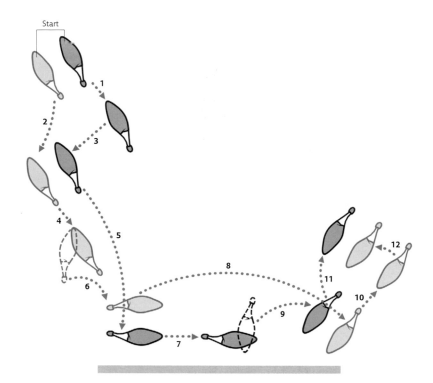

Lady's Steps

Start by backing slightly out of the room in a backwards direction, referred to as 'backing diagonally to wall' by dancers.

one   **1 Right foot** takes a step backwards.

two   **2 Left foot** takes a step to side on the same line as the right foot.

three   **3 Right foot** closes to left foot.

one   **4 Left foot** takes a step backwards, beginning to turn to the right.

two   **5 Right foot** takes a step to the side, still turning to the right.

three   **6 Left foot** closes to right foot still turning to right. Your right shoulder should now be pointing towards the nearest wall.

one   **7 Right foot** takes a step forwards, still turning to right.

two   **8 Left foot** takes a step to the side, still turning to the right.

three   **9 Right foot** closes to left foot, completing the turn to the right. You should now be 'backing diagonally to centre'.

one   **10 Left foot** takes a step backwards.

two   **11 Right foot** takes a step to the side on the same line as left foot.

three   **12 Left foot** closes to right foot, 'backing diagonally to centre'.

Right or Natural Turn

1
count: one

M Left foot takes a step forwards.

L Right foot takes a step backwards.

2
count: two

M Right foot takes a step to the side on the same line as the left foot.

L Left foot takes a step to the side on the same line as the right foot.

5
count: two

M Left foot takes a step to the side, still turning to the right.

L Right foot takes a step to the side, still turning to the right.

6
count: three

M Right foot closes to left foot, still turning to the right.

L Left foot closes to right foot, still turning to the right.

3

count: three

M Left foot closes to right foot.

L Right foot closes to left foot.

4

count: one

M Right foot takes a step forwards, beginning to turn to the right.

L Left foot takes a step backwards, beginning to turn to the right.

7

count: one

M Left foot takes a step backwards, still turning to the right.

L Right foot takes a step forwards, still turning to the right.

8

count: two

M Right foot takes a step to the side, still turning to the right.

L Left foot takes a step to the side, still turning to the right.

(continued overleaf)

Right or Natural Turn (continued)

9

count: three

M Left foot closes to right foot, completing the turn to the right.

L Right foot closes to left foot, completing the turn to the right.

10

count: one

M Right foot takes a step forwards.

L Left foot takes a step backwards.

11

count: two

M Left foot takes a step to the side on same line as right foot.

L Right foot takes a step to the side on same line as left foot.

12

count: three

M Right foot closes to left foot.

L Left foot closes to right foot.

The Whisk, Chassé and Right or Natural Turn

This grouping can follow the Left or Reverse Turn. Stepping 'outside partner' is introduced here – a step is taken to one side of your partner.

Man's Steps

count:

Start by 'facing diagonally to wall'.

one **1 Left foot** takes a step forwards, starting to increase pressure of the heel of your right hand on lady's back.

two **2 Right foot** takes a step to the side, turning partner so that she turns her right side away from your left side, you do not turn. The lead should come from your right hand.

three **3 Left foot** crosses loosely behind right foot, continuing to lead the lady to complete her turn, so that she finishes with her right side roughly 30 cm (11¾ in) away from your hip in promenade position.

one **4 Right foot** takes a step forwards and across left foot along a line parallel with the nearest wall, still in promenade position.

two **5 Left foot** takes a step to the side along the line parallel with the wall, starting to increase pressure of fingers of right hand on the lady's back, taking half a beat of music.

and **6 Right foot** closes to left foot, continuing to press on lady's back with right finger tips to bring her back to face you, taking half a beat of music.

three **7 Left foot** takes a step to the side, still moving along a line parallel with nearest wall. The lady should now be facing you.

one **8 Right foot** takes a step forwards to your left of your partner's feet, 'outside partner', starting to turn to the right.

two **9 Left foot** takes a step to the side, still turning right, and as this step is taken your partner comes into line with you again.

three **10 Right foot** closes to left foot, still turning right, your left shoulder should be pointing towards the nearest wall – 'backing line of dance'.

one **11 Left foot** takes a step backwards, still turning to the right.

two **12 Right foot** takes a step to the side, still turning to the right.

three **13 Left foot** closes to right foot, completing the turn to the right, you should now be 'facing diagonally to centre'.

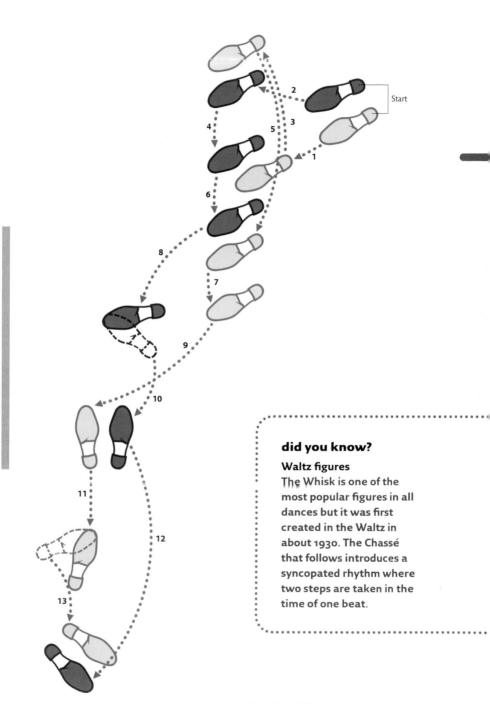

Start

did you know?

Waltz figures
The Whisk is one of the most popular figures in all dances but it was first created in the Waltz in about 1930. The Chassé that follows introduces a syncopated rhythm where two steps are taken in the time of one beat.

The Whisk, Chassé and Right or Natural Turn (continued)

Lady's Steps

Start by 'backing diagonally to wall'.

count:

one   **1** **Right foot** takes a step backwards.

two   **2** **Left foot** takes a step to the side, turning your right side away from man's left side.

three   **3** **Right foot** crosses loosely behind left foot, continuing to turn so that you finish with your right side roughly 30 cm (11¾ in) away from your partner's hip in promenade position.

one   **4** **Left foot** takes a step forwards and across right foot along a line parallel with the nearest wall, commencing to turn to left, still in promenade position.

two   **5** **Right foot** takes a step to the side along the line parallel with the wall, still turning to the left, taking half a beat of music.

and   **6** **Left foot** closes to right foot, continuing to turn to the left, you should now be facing the man, taking half a beat of music.

three   **7** **Right foot** takes a step to the side, still moving along a line parallel with nearest wall.

one   **8** **Left foot** takes a step backwards and your partner steps to the right of your feet, 'outside partner', starting to turn to the right.

two   **9** **Right foot** takes a step to the side, still turning right, and as this step is taken your partner comes into line with you again.

three   **10** **Left foot** closes to right foot, still turning, your right shoulder should be pointing towards the nearest wall, that is, 'facing line of dance'.

one   **11** **Right foot** takes a step forwards, still turning to the right.

two   **12** **Left foot** takes a step to the side, still turning to the right.

three   **13** **Right foot** closes to left foot still turning to the right, you should now be 'backing diagonally to centre'.

watch out!

Pressure on the back
In turning the lady into the whisk position the man guides her by increasing the pressure with the heel of his right hand on her back. There is an understandable instinct to turn the lady by pushing her right hand back with your left hand. This must be resisted.

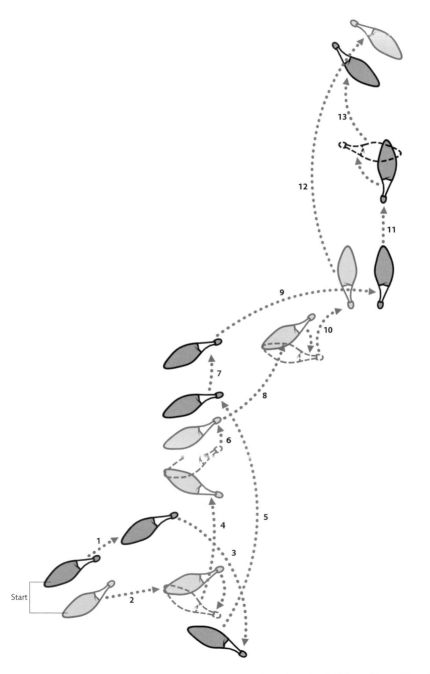

Start

1

2

3

4

5

6

7

8

9

10

11

12

13

The Whisk, Chassé and Right or Natural Turn

The Whisk

1

count: one

M Left foot takes a step forwards, starting to increase pressure of the heel of right hand on lady's back.

L Right foot takes a step backwards.

2

count: two

M Right foot takes a step to the side, turning your partner with right hand.

L Left foot takes a step to the side, turning right side away from man's left side.

The Chassé

4

count: one

M Right foot forwards and across left foot, parallel with the wall.

L Left foot forwards and across right foot, parallel with the wall, starting to turn to left.

5

count: two

M Left foot steps to the side, parallel with the wall.

L Right foot steps to the side, parallel with the wall, still turning to the left. Takes half a beat of music.

3

count: three

M Left foot crosses loosely behind right foot, still leading the lady.

L Right foot crosses loosely behind left foot, still turning to promenade position.

must know

Don't be shy
When turning into whisk position the lady should resist any shyness she may have, stretch the neck and body muscles, carry her head further back and, in the nicest of ways, flaunt herself a little.

6

count: and

M Right foot closes to left foot, continuing to press on lady's back.

L Left foot closes to right foot, still turning to to the left. You should now be facing the man. Takes half a beat of music.

7

count: three

M Left foot takes a step to the side along a line parallel with the wall.

L Right foot takes a step to the side, still moving along a line parallel with the wall.

(continued overleaf)

The Whisk, Chassé and Right or Natural Turn | 75

The Whisk, Chassé and Right or Natural Turn (continued)

Right or Natural Turn

8
count: one

M Right foot steps forwards to your left of partner's feet, 'outside partner', turning to the right.

L Left foot steps backwards starting to turn to the right.

9
count: two

M Left foot takes a step to the side, still turning to right, partner comes into line with you again.

L Right foot takes a step to the side, still turning to the right.

11
count: one

M Left foot takes a step backwards, still turning to the right.

L Right foot takes a step forwards, still turning to the right.

12
count: two

M Right foot takes a step to the side, still turning to the right.

L Left foot takes a step to the side, still turning to the right.

10

count: three

M Right foot closes to left foot, still turning to the right and 'backing line of dance'.

L Left foot closes to right foot, turning right and 'facing line of dance'.

13

count: three

M Left foot closes to right foot, completing the turn to the right.

L Right foot closes to left foot, completing the turn to the right.

want to know more?

• Visit the local library and take out instructional books on ballroom dancing. Some will include dance figures not featured in this book.
• Watch ballroom dance programmes on TV, such as 'Strictly Come Dancing', paying particular attention to the comments of judges who have B.D.C. recognized qualifications.
• Join a dance school. See listing of dance studios on pages 184–9, and check with your local authority for evening classes.
• Buy the CD 'Take Your Partners Please – Waltz' by Ray Hamilton, from The Ballroom Collection.

weblinks

• BBC's 'Strictly Come Dancing': www.bbc.co.uk /strictlycomedancing/
• For a website dedicated to competitive dance: www.dancesport.uk.com /index.htm

4 Quickstep

This is a joyful dance full of verve and vitality, which will appeal to the more energetic of you. It developed from the Foxtrot, which became popular in the USA in the jazz era. The dance took two basic forms, Quick and Slow Foxtrots. The quick version was heavily influenced by the Charleston, and in the 1920s the 'Quicktime Foxtrot and Charleston' was one of the dances featured in a professional championship Shortly after this the name 'Quickstep' was coined and the Charleston influence waned – although good dancers will still introduce some Charleston figures into their dance.

A fast-tempo dance

The Quickstep is a British dance that developed from American dances in the post-World War I years. It is a derivative of the Foxtrot, which came to the fore in the USA in 1914.

The Foxtrot can, in turn, be traced to the One Step and Castle Walk of the years immediately pre-World War I.

The Castle Walk was named after Irene and Vernon Castle, who were highly regarded dancers in the years preceding the War. Vernon Castle was British, born in Norwich as Vernon Blyth, before he adopted the name Castle. He emigrated to the USA where he married Irene. When war broke out, he returned to England to volunteer for the Royal Air Force. Sadly he was killed in an air crash.

In Britain, the Castle Walk developed into two versions, one quick and one slow. In due course, following modifications, one has become our Quickstep and the other the Slow Foxtrot. The latter is a particularly British development, although it did have some American input. The basis of the modern Slow Foxtrot was laid in the early 1920s and prominent in its development and promotion were Britain's Queen of the Ballroom, Josephine Bradley, and Mr G. K. Anderson, who was an American amateur dancer. (See the chapter on the Slow Foxtrot, pages 148–81.)

Fast version

The early version of a fast Foxtrot was known, in Britain, as the Quick-Time Foxtrot and Charleston, but in a short space of time it became known as the Quickstep. In the USA, a very fast version of the Foxtrot became known as the Peabody, or the Roseland Foxtrot. It is still danced stateside under the name of Peabody. The name comes from police lieutenant William Frank Peabody, from Brooklyn, who helped to popularize the dance.

The dance has progressed and is now more lively. Experienced dancers can make use of Polka rhythms, Charleston, skipping steps and fast syncopation movements. You may have seen on television expert dancers, such as Anton du Beke and Erin Boag, make full use of the scope given to them by the dance. However, do not assume that the dance is only for the skilled. The Quickstep is a simple dance and one that everyone can enjoy, and because it is fairly quick at 48–50 bars a minute, it provides you with excellent exercise. It is more energetic than walking, and to dance the Quickstep for about ten to fifteen minutes will probably give you as much exercise as walking one mile. Add to that the discipline of learning the steps, and applying what you have learnt, and you have a healthy exercise programme.

A demonstration, by an experienced ballroom dancing couple, of the intricate footwork needed for the Quickstep, along with their elaborate costumes.

Hold and time
This is a dance which uses a Close Hold (see pages 14–15). The music is in 4/4 time (four beats to the bar) and individual steps take up either one or two beats of music.

Chassés Progressing

This preparatory exercise is included in order to get you used to the feel of the rhythm and the type of patterns used in the Quickstep. The eight steps, not including the preparatory step, can be repeated.

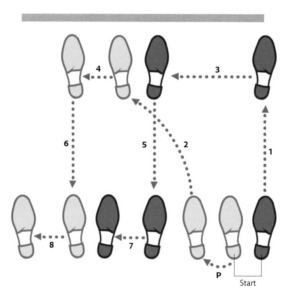

count: **Man's Steps**

Start by facing the nearest wall.

slow **P** **Left foot** takes a small step to the side, taking two beats of music.

slow **1** **Right foot** takes a step forwards, taking two beats of music.

quick **2** **Left foot** takes a step to the side along the line parallel with the wall that the right foot is on, taking one beat of music.

quick **3** **Right foot** closes to left foot, with the weight back onto right foot, taking one beat of music.

slow **4** **Left foot** takes a small step to the side, taking two beats of music.

slow **5** **Right foot** takes a step backwards, taking two beats of music.

quick **6** **Left foot** takes a step to the side along the line parallel with wall that the right foot is on, taking one beat of music.

quick **7** **Right foot** closes to left foot, taking one beat of music.

slow **8** **Left foot** takes a small step to the side, taking two beats of music.

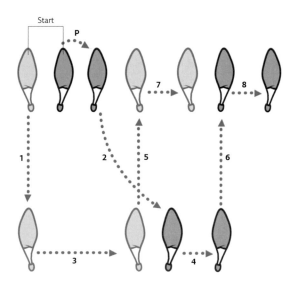

count: ## Lady's Steps

Start by backing the nearest wall.

slow **P** **Right foot** takes a small step to the side, taking two beats of music.

slow **1** **Left foot** takes a step backwards, taking two beats of music.

quick **2** **Right foot** takes a step to the side along the line parallel with the wall that the left foot is on, taking one beat of music.

quick **3** **Left foot** closes to right foot, with the weight back onto the left foot, taking one beat of music.

slow **4** **Right foot** takes a small step to the side, taking two beats of music.

slow **5** **Left foot** takes a step forwards, taking two beats of music.

quick **6** **Right foot** takes a step to the side along the line parallel with wall that the left foot is on, taking one beat of music.

quick **7** **Left foot** closes to right foot, taking one beat of music.

slow **8** **Right foot** takes a small step to the side, taking two beats of music.

Chassés Progressing

P

count: slow

M Left foot takes a small step to the side.

L Right foot takes a small step to the side.

Takes two beats of music.

1

count: slow

M Right foot takes a step forwards.

L Left foot takes a step backwards.

Takes two beats of music.

2

count: quick

M Left foot takes a step to the side.

L Right foot takes a step to the side.

Takes one beat of music.

5

count: slow

M Right foot takes a step backwards.

L Left foot takes a step forwards.

Takes two beats of music.

6

count: quick

M Left foot takes a step to the side.

L Right foot takes a step to the side.

Takes one beat of music.

must know

Quick feet
The eight steps shown here, not including the preparatory step, can be repeated.

You might find it helpful to remember the foot patterns rather than count in Slows and Quicks. The man should count to himself 'forward, side, close, side, backward, side, close, side'. The lady should count 'backward, side, close, side, forward, side, close, side'.

3
count: quick

M Right foot closes to left foot.

L Left foot closes to right foot.

Takes one beat of music.

4
count: slow

M Left foot takes a small step to the side.

L Right foot takes a small step to the side.

Takes two beats of music.

7
count: quick

M Right foot closes to left foot.

L Left foot closes to right foot.

Takes one beat of music.

8
count: slow

M Left foot takes a small step to the side.

L Right foot takes a small step to the side.

Takes two beats of music.

Quarter Turn and Progressive Chassé

This figure is similar to the Chassés Progressing but with a little turn to the right and left. When it is repeated, the man takes step 1 'outside partner'.

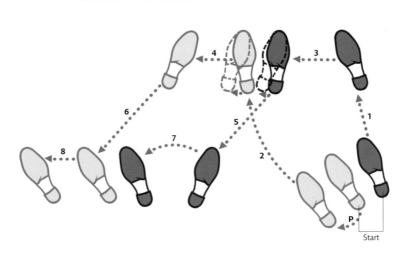

Man's Steps

count:

Start by facing the nearest wall and then turn left about 45 degrees – 'facing diagonally to wall'.

slow **P** **Left foot** takes a small step to the side.

slow **1** **Right foot** takes a step forwards, starting to turn right.

quick **2** **Left foot** takes a step to the side, turning to the right.

quick **3** **Right foot** closes to left foot, still turning to the right.

slow **4** **Left foot** takes a small step to the side. You should have turned about a quarter of a turn to the right and be facing slanting out of the room against the direction of the dance ('backing diagonally to centre').

slow **5** **Right foot** takes a step backwards, starting to turn to the left.

quick **6** **Left foot** takes a step to the side, turning to the left.

quick **7** **Right foot** closes to left foot, still turning to the left.

slow **8** **Left foot** takes a small step to the side. You should have turned about a quarter of a turn to the left and be 'facing diagonally to wall' again.

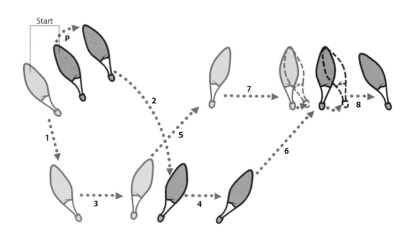

Lady's Steps

Start with your back towards the nearest wall and then turn left about 45 degrees – 'backing diagonally to wall'.

slow **P** **Right foot** takes a small step to the side.

slow **1** **Left foot** takes a step backwards, starting to turn right.

quick **2** **Right foot** takes a step to the side, turning to the right.

quick **3** **Left foot** closes to right foot, still turning to the right.

slow **4** **Right foot** takes a small step to the side. You should have turned about a quarter of a turn to the right and be facing slanting into the room and in the direction of the dance ('facing diagonally to centre').

slow **5** **Left foot** takes a step forwards, starting to turn to the left.

quick **6** **Right foot** takes a step to the side, turning to the left.

quick **7** **Left foot** closes to right foot, still turning to the left.

slow **8** **Right foot** takes a small step to the side. You should have turned about a quarter of a turn to the left and be 'backing diagonally to wall' again.

Quarter Turn and Progressive Chassé

P
count: slow

M Left foot takes a small step to the side.

L Right foot takes a small step to the side.

1
count: slow

M Right foot takes a small step forwards, starting to turn right.

L Left foot takes a small step backwards, starting to turn right.

2
count: quick

M Left foot takes a step to the side, turning to the right.

L Right foot takes a step to the side, turning to the right.

5
count: slow

M Right foot takes a step backwards, starting to turn to the left.

L Left foot takes a step forwards, starting to turn to the left.

6
count: quick

M Left foot takes a step to the side, turning to the left.

L Right foot takes a step to the side, turning to the left.

3
count: quick

M Right foot
closes to left
foot, still
turning to
the right.

L Left foot
closes to right
foot still
turning to
the right.

4
count: slow

M Left foot takes
a small step to
side, completing
the turn to
the right.

L Right foot takes
a small step to
side, completing
the turn to
the right.

7
count: quick

M Right foot
closes to left
foot, still
turning to
the left.

L Left foot
closes to right
foot, still
turning to
the left.

8
count: slow

M Left foot
takes a small
step to side,
completing
the turn to
the left.

L Right foot
takes a small
step to side,
completing
the turn to
the left.

The Forward Lock Step

This is a very popular figure and is ideally followed by any figure commencing on the man's right foot stepping 'outside partner'. For example, the Quarter Turn and Progressive Chassé (see pages 86–9), or Natural Pivot Turn (see pages 98–101), omitting the preparatory steps in both of these figures.

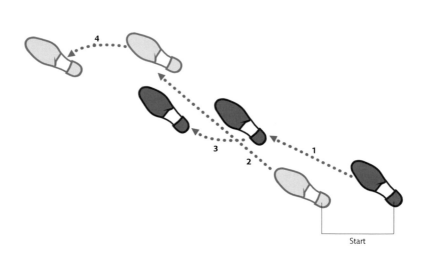

Start

Man's Steps

count:

Start by 'facing diagonally to wall'.

slow 1 **Right foot** takes a step forwards to your left of both your partner's feet, 'outside partner', onto the heel of your foot.

quick 2 **Left foot** takes a step forwards, leading with the left side of your body a little and stepping onto the ball of foot, rather than heel.

quick 3 **Right foot** crosses behind left foot, stepping onto the ball of your right foot so that the weight is carried on the balls of both feet.

slow 4 **Left foot** takes a small step forwards and to the side, still on the balls of your feet, lowering the heel at the end of the step.

must know

What's in a name
The Quickstep is an energetic
dance and is danced to fast-tempo
4/4 music. Although the rhythm
is the same as that for the Slow
Foxtrot, it is a much quicker tempo.

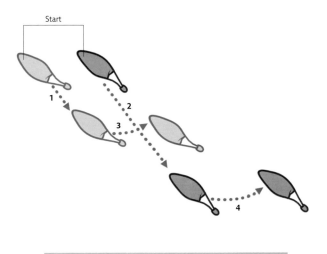

Lady's Steps

count:

Start by 'backing diagonally to wall'.

slow 1 Left foot takes a small step
backwards with your partner
stepping to the right of both
your feet, 'outside partner'.

quick 2 Right foot takes a step backwards,
leading with the right side of your
body a little and not lowering the
heel of your foot as the weight is
taken onto it.

quick 3 Left foot crosses in front of right
foot, stepping onto the ball of your
left foot so that the weight is carried
on the balls of both feet.

slow 4 Right foot takes a small step
backwards and to the side, still on
the balls of your feet, lowering the
heel at the end of the step.

The Forward Lock Step

1

count: slow

M **Right foot** takes a small step forwards, 'outside partner', onto the heel of your foot.

L **Left foot** takes a small step backwards, 'partner outside', lowering heel.

2

count: quick

M **Left foot** forwards, leading with left side and stepping onto the ball of your foot.

L **Right foot** backwards, leading with right side, and heel is not lowered.

3

count: quick

M **Right foot** crosses behind left foot, weight is on the balls of both feet.

L **Left foot** crosses in front of right foot, weight is on the balls of both feet.

4

count: slow

M **Left foot** forwards and to the side.

L **Right foot** backwards and to the side.

Both man and lady still on balls of feet, lowering heels at the end of the step.

Quick Open Reverse Turn with Progressive Chassé Ending

When it is not danced at a corner, precede this figure with a Quarter Turn and Progressive Chassé (see pages 86–9) turned strongly to the left to finish 'facing diagonally to centre', then follow with a forwards step on the man's right foot.

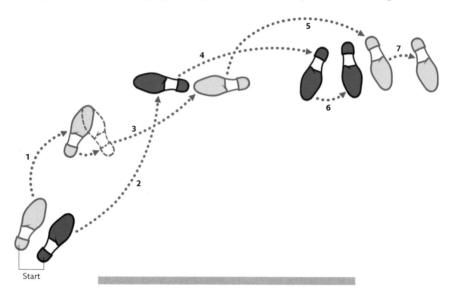

Start

Man's Steps

count:

Start by 'facing diagonally to centre'.

slow 1 **Left foot** takes a step forwards, turning to the left.

quick 2 **Right foot** takes a small step to the side, still turning to the left.

quick 3 **Left foot** takes a step backwards, still turning left and leading the lady to step to the right of both your feet, 'partner outside'. You should now be facing down the room against the direction of the dance (left shoulder pointing towards the nearest wall).

slow 4 **Right foot** takes a step backwards, still turning to the left.

quick 5 **Left foot** takes a step to the side, still turning to the left, now facing the nearest wall.

quick 6 **Right foot** closes to left foot, completing the turn to the left.

slow 7 **Left foot** takes a small step to the side, preparing to step 'outside partner' on the next step.

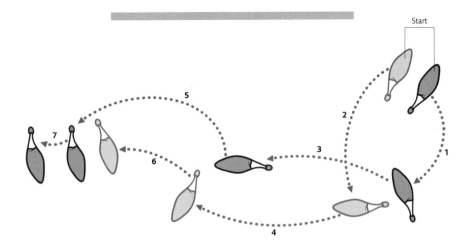

Lady's Steps

Start by 'backing diagonally to centre'.

slow 1 Right foot takes a step backwards, turning to the left.

quick 2 Left foot takes a step to the side, still turning to the left.

quick 3 Right foot takes a step forwards, still turning left and stepping to your left of both your partner's feet, 'outside partner'. You should now be facing down the room in the direction of the dance (right shoulder pointing towards the nearest wall).

slow 4 Left foot takes a step forwards, still turning to the left.

quick 5 Right foot takes a step to the side, still turning left, now with back towards the nearest wall.

quick 6 Left foot closes to right foot, completing the turn to the left.

slow 7 Right foot takes a small step to the side.

Quick Open Reverse Turn with Progressive Chassé Ending

1

count: slow

M **Left foot** takes a step forwards, turning to the left.

L **Right foot** takes a step backwards, turning to the left.

2

count: quick

M **Right foot** takes a step to the side, still turning to left.

L **Left foot** takes a step to the side, still turning to left.

5

count: quick

M **Left foot** a step to side, still turning left, now facing nearest wall.

L **Right foot** a step to side, still turning left, now with back towards nearest wall.

6

count: quick

M **Right foot** closes to left foot, completing turn to left.

L **Left foot** closes to right foot, completing turn to left.

3

count: quick

M Left foot backwards, still turning to the left, leading lady to step 'outside partner'.

L Right foot forwards, still turning to the left.

4

count: slow

M Right foot takes a step backwards, still turning to the left.

L Left foot takes a step forwards, still turning to the left.

7

count: slow

M Left foot takes a small step to the side, preparing to step 'outside partner' on the next step.

L Right foot takes a small step to the side.

must know

The next step
Follow this figure with either a Quarter Turn and Progressive Chassé, a Natural Pivot Turn or a Forward Lock Step, commencing with the man's right foot taking a small step forwards to his left of the lady's feet, that is, 'outside partner'.

The Natural Pivot Turn

This figure is useful when you are approaching a corner, because when you have completed it, you are in a position to move along the next side of the room. It is a little more difficult, but is a very valuable dancing asset and worth a little extra effort. Follow this figure with the Quarter Turn and Progressive Chassé (see pages 86–9), omitting the preparatory step.

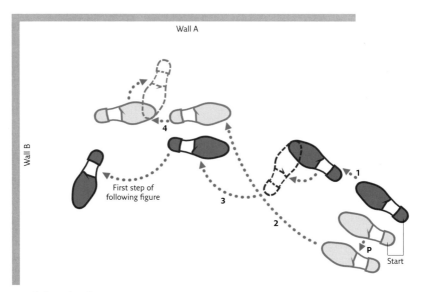

Man's Steps

count:

Start by 'facing diagonally to wall A', that is, stand with your right side or shoulder pointing towards the nearest wall and turn 45 degrees to your right.

slow P Left foot takes a small step to the side.

slow 1 Right foot takes a step forwards, turning to the right.

quick 2 Left foot takes a step to the side, still turning to the right.

quick 3 Right foot closes to left foot, still turning to the right. By now your left side should be pointing towards wall A and your back should be backing wall B.

slow 4 Left foot takes a step backwards and leftwards, turning strongly to the right on the ball of your foot, but with your heel close to the floor and leaving your right foot forwards in front of your left foot. Turn sufficiently so that you are now 'facing diagonally to wall B'.

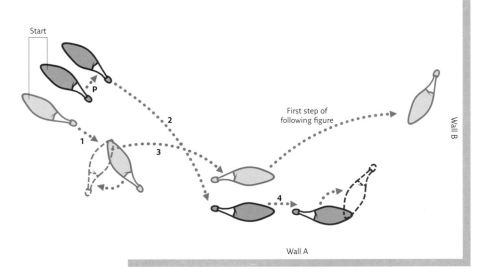

Start

P

2

1

3

First step of
following figure

4

Wall B

Wall A

<table>
<tr><td>count:</td><td colspan="2">

Lady's Steps
</td></tr>
</table>

Start by 'backing diagonally to wall
A', that is, stand with your left side
or shoulder pointing towards the
nearest wall and turn 45 degrees to
your right.

slow **P** **Right foot** takes a small step to
the side.

slow **1** **Left foot** takes a step backwards,
turning to the right.

quick **2** **Right foot** takes a step to the side,
still turning to right.

quick **3** **Left foot** closes to right foot, still
turning to the right. By now your
right side should be pointing
towards wall A and you should be
facing wall B.

slow **4** **Right foot** takes a step forwards,
turning strongly to the right on the
ball of your foot, but with your heel
close to the floor and leaving your
left foot backwards behind your
right foot. Turn sufficiently so that
you are now 'backing diagonally
to wall B'.

The Natural Pivot Turn

P
count: slow

M Left foot takes a small step to the side.

L Right foot takes a small step to the side.

1
count: slow

M Right foot takes a step forwards, turning to the right.

L Left foot takes a step backwards, turning to the right.

3
count: quick

M Right foot closes to left foot, still turning to the right.

L Left foot closes to right foot still turning to the right.

4
count: slow

M Left foot takes a step backwards and to the left, turning strongly to the right.

L Right foot takes a step forwards, turning strongly to the right.

2
count: quick

M Left foot takes
a step to side,
still turning to
the right.

L Right foot takes
a step to side,
still turning to
the right.

F
finish

Position reached
after the strong
turn to the right.
Both man and
lady finish facing
a little to the
right of a line
running parallel
to the new wall.

want to know more?
• Subscribe to one of the
specialist journals. Choose
from: *Dance Expression*
(monthly), *Dance News*
(weekly – newspaper
format), *Dance Today*
(monthly).
• Join a dance school. For
addresses, look in local
newspapers, *Yellow Pages*
and see Dance studios on
pages 184-9.
• Check with your local
authority for evening
classes.
• For inspiration, hire a
video of the film *Top Hat*,
starring Fred Astaire and
Ginger Rogers.

weblinks
• Get a taste of what
Dance Today magazine
contains: www.dancing-
times.co.uk/dancetoday
• For mail order specialist
dance music, C & D Dance
Records: www.freewebs.
com/candddance
• See pages 183-4 for
websites of dance
teachers' organizations.

5 Rock 'n' Roll and Jive

These dances represent two sides of the same coin and are the exuberant and ebullient expression of the joy of life by the young at heart. The Jitterbug – a very energetic dance form – arrived in Britain with the American GIs during World War II; two variants of the dance, Rock 'n' Roll and Jive, developed. You will see Jive in dance competitions and its 'quick a quick' rhythms take on a twinkling form. While Rock 'n' Roll with its strong emphasis on the 'off' beats in common time music creates a more 'gutsy' expression.

Rhythm-and-blues roots

The majority of popular dances, if not all, develop from the dancing public and are not generally an invention of any one person. It is a strange process and difficult to track down.

Rock 'n' Roll music has its roots in rhythm-and-blues, which was first played by black musicians in the USA in the late 1920s. Later, in the mid-1930s, the Boswell Sisters had success with the song 'Rock and Roll' – predating the phenomenon of Rock 'n' Roll by nearly 20 years. Similarly, 'Rock it for Me' was recorded by several bands in 1937 and dancers began to exploit the positive rhythms. The impact of these trends was felt when American Forces were based in Britain during World War II. Their presence transformed the ballrooms, which began to promote energetic big bands, encouraging wild dancing and virtuoso improvisation. For the safety of dancers it was necessary to place some restrictions on what dancers could perform. Some dancehalls even carried notices stating 'No Jitterbugging'.

Jive to rock

Rock 'n' Roll was gradually becoming acceptable and dance teachers codified the dance, using the name Jive. With the success of a new breed of dance band – the rock group – Rock 'n' Roll was firmly established. Prior to the post-War years, bands had been fairly large, commonly up to 14 musicians who played melodious tunes. The rock bands were smaller, concentrated more on rhythm instruments and with less emphasis on tune.

The greatest impact was that of Bill Haley and the Comets with their recording of 'Rock Around The Clock' in 1954. When they appeared in theatres, the aisles were full of youngsters dancing. Elvis Presley cemented the original impact with tunes such as 'All Shook Up'. Many popular modern music tunes, with

Dancehall owners in the 1950s tried to ban this sort of acrobatic Jive so as to avoid possible harm to other dancers.

their emphasis on heavy, insistent rhythms, are excellent for Rock 'n' Roll and Jive, as well as other variants now to be seen.

Rock 'n' Roll rhythms

When the dance was first analysed, three optional rhythms were identified that can be characterized as single, double and triple step types. Jive uses the triple rhythm unit while Rock 'n' Roll uses the single. The different rhythms (units) create a distinctive character for each dance. However, nearly all figures in one style can be danced in the other and vice versa.

Firstly, some figures in Rock 'n' Roll rhythm are described and, secondly, it is shown how they can be danced in Jive. The Rock 'n' Roll format has been chosen as the starting form because it is believed to be slightly easier, and is most favoured by social dancers. There may be places where the instructions given contradict the technique accepted by most dance authorities. Instructions have been written in such a way as to make the figures easy for the beginner.

The hold

This is a relaxed dance with a casual Open Hold. Because there is no body contact, it is important to remember that the guide from the man has to come through his hands.

Rock 'n' Roll Rhythm Basic

There is very little movement across the floor over these steps and each group of three steps is rather like a shuffle. The important aspect is to try to feel the accents in the music on the second and fourth beats of the bar and express them with extra pressure into the floor when possible. The quick steps in Rock 'n' Roll take one beat of music and the slow steps take two beats. Start in Open Hold.

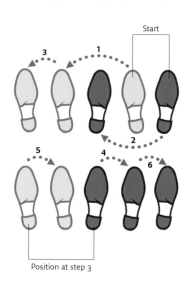

Position at step 3

Man's Steps

count:

quick **1** Left foot takes a step to the left, taking one beat of music.

quick **2** Right foot closes towards the left foot, taking one beat of music.

slow **3** Left foot takes a tiny step to the left, increasing the pressure on the foot during the second half of the step, taking two beats of music.

quick **4** Right foot takes a tiny step to the right, taking one beat of music.

quick **5** Left foot closes towards the right foot, taking one beat of music.

slow **6** Right foot takes a tiny step to the right, increasing the pressure on the foot during the second half of the step, taking two beats of music.

Open Hold

For Rock 'n' Roll and Jive, use a casual Open Hold. Stand about 15–20 cm (6–8 in) away from each other. The man holds the lady with his right hand on her back just below her left shoulder blade and with the heel of his hand almost on the side of her body. He holds her right hand loosely in his left hand at a little below shoulder level or lower. The lady rests her left hand on the upper part of the man's right arm.

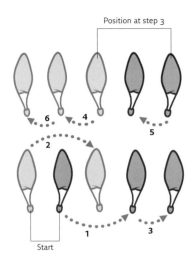

Position at step 3

Start

count: ## Lady's Steps

quick **1** Right foot takes a step to the right, taking one beat of music.

quick **2** Left foot closes towards the right foot, taking one beat of music.

slow **3** Right foot takes a tiny step to the right, increasing the pressure on the foot during second half of the step, taking two beats of music.

quick **4** Left foot takes a tiny step to the left, taking one beat of music.

quick **5** Right foot closes towards the left foot, taking one beat of music.

slow **6** Left foot takes a tiny step to the left, increasing the pressure on the foot during the second half of the step, taking two beats of music.

Rock 'n' Roll Rhythm Basic

1

count: quick

M Left foot takes a step to the left.

L Right foot takes a step to the right.

2

count: quick

M Right foot closes towards the left foot.

L Left foot closes towards the right foot.

3

count: slow

M Left foot takes a tiny step to left, increasing pressure on foot.

L Right foot takes a tiny step to right, increasing pressure on foot.

4

count: quick

M Right foot takes a tiny step to the right.

L Left foot takes a tiny step to the left.

5

count: quick

M Left foot closes towards the right foot.

L Right foot closes towards the left foot.

6

count: slow

M Right foot takes a tiny step to right, increasing pressure on foot.

L Left foot takes a tiny step to left, increasing pressure on foot.

Fall-away Rhythm Basic

Once you have danced the first six steps of the Rock 'n' Roll Rhythm Basic (see pages 106–9) you can follow it with Fall-away Rhythm Basic. These four steps can be repeated as often as you fancy. Commence in Open Hold (see page 107) .

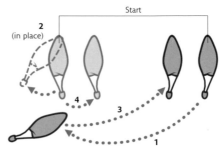

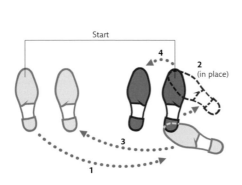

count:	Man's Steps
quick	**1** Left foot takes a step backwards, turning to the left so that your left side moves away from the lady's right side, making a V shape.
quick	**2** Right foot remains in place and weight is taken firmly forwards onto it, starting to turn right to face your partner again.
slow	**3** Left foot takes a small step to the side, turning right to face your partner, increasing pressure on foot during the second half of the step.
slow	**4** Right foot takes a tiny step towards the left foot, increasing pressure on the foot at the end of the step.

count:	Lady's Steps
quick	**1** Right foot takes a step backwards, turning to the right so that your right side moves away from the man's left side, making a V shape.
quick	**2** Left foot remains in place and weight is taken firmly forwards onto it, beginning to turn left to face towards partner again.
slow	**3** Right foot takes a small step to the side, turning left to face your partner, increasing pressure on foot during the second half of the step.
slow	**4** Left foot takes a tiny step towards the right foot, increasing pressure on the foot during the second half of the step.

1

count: quick

M Left foot backwards, turning to the left.

L Right foot backwards turning to the right so that your right side moves away from the man's left side.

2

count: quick

M Right foot remains in place, taking weight onto it, starting to turn right.

L Left foot remains in place, taking weight onto it, starting to turn left to face towards partner.

3

count: slow

M Left foot takes a small step to the side, turning to right, with pressure on foot.

L Right foot takes a small step to the side, turning to left to face partner, with pressure on foot.

4

count: slow

M Right foot takes a tiny step towards left foot, with pressure on foot.

L Left foot takes a tiny step towards right foot, with pressure on foot.

Underarm Turn to Right for Lady

Dance this figure after the Rhythm Basic (see pages 106–9) or the Fall-away Rhythm Basic (see pages 110–11); follow this with the Link (see pages 114–15).

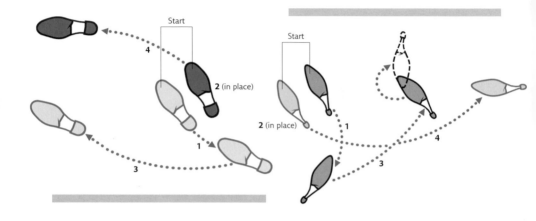

Man's Steps

count:

quick 1 Left foot takes a step backwards, turning to the left so that your left side moves further away from the lady's right side, making a small V shape.

quick 2 Right foot remains in place, weight is taken firmly forwards onto it. Start turning the lady a little to her left by pressure with the right hand and begin to raise your left hand.

slow 3 Left foot takes a small step to the side, then turning to your left after a brief pause, turn the lady to her right under your left and her right hand. Do not grip the lady's hand too tightly but allow her to turn.

slow 4 Right foot takes a small step to the side, completing the turn to your left.

Lady's Steps

count:

quick 1 Right foot takes a step backwards, turning to the right so that your right side moves further away from the man's left side, making a small V shape.

quick 2 Left foot remains in place, weight is taken firmly forwards onto it and start turning a little to your left.

slow 3 Right foot takes a step to the side, turning to the left but with your right side still away from your partner. Press into the floor and spin on the ball of your right foot about three quarters of a full turn to the right to face your partner.

slow 4 Left foot takes a small step backwards, completing the turn to your right.

1

count: quick

M Left foot backwards, turning to left, moving away from lady's right side.

L Right foot backwards. turning to right, moving away from man's left side.

2

count: quick

M Right foot remains in place, weight taken onto it, turning lady to left. Start to raise left hand.

L Left foot remains in place, weight taken onto it, start turning to the left.

3

count: slow

M Left foot a step to side, turning lady to her right.

L Right foot a step to the side turning left, then spin on the ball of your foot to the right until you face your partner.

4

count: slow

M Right foot takes a small step to the side, turning to your left.

L Left foot takes a small step backwards, completing the turn to your right.

The Link

This figure brings partners together in normal hold with the man holding the lady's right hand in his left hand, after they have been separated. The man stands with the weight on his right foot and the lady with the weight on her left foot. Dance the Link after the Underarm Turn to Right for Lady (see pages 112–13).

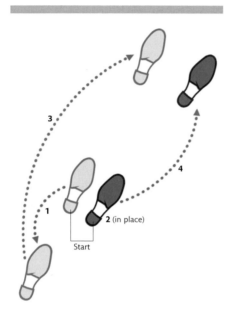

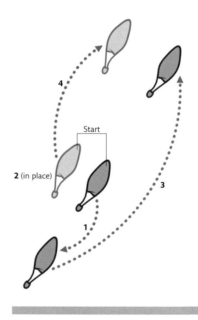

count:		**Man's Steps**
quick	1	**Left foot** takes a small step backwards.
quick	2	**Right foot** remains in place and weight is taken firmly forwards onto it.
slow	3	**Left foot** takes a small step forwards, drawing partner towards you to regain normal hold.
slow	4	**Right foot** takes a small step to the side in normal hold.

count:		**Lady's Steps**
quick	1	**Right foot** takes a small step backwards.
quick	2	**Left foot** remains in place and weight is taken firmly forwards onto it.
slow	3	**Right foot** takes a small step forwards towards partner, to regain normal hold.
slow	4	**Left foot** takes a small step to the side in normal hold.

1

count: quick

M Left foot takes a small step backwards.

L Right foot takes a small step backwards.

2

count: quick

M Right foot remains in place and weight is taken firmly forwards onto it.

L Left foot remains in place and weight is taken firmly forwards onto it.

3

count: slow

M Left foot takes a small step forwards, drawing the lady towards you to regain normal hold.

L Right foot takes a small step forwards, to regain normal hold.

4

count: slow

M Right foot takes a small step to the side in normal hold.

L Left foot takes a small step to the side in normal hold.

The Link in Jive Rhythm

All of the Rock 'n' Roll figures can be danced with Jive Rhythm. Whenever a step is counted 'slow', replace that step with three by counting 'quick a quick'. The precise beat value is ¾, ¼, 1, making two beats of common time music.

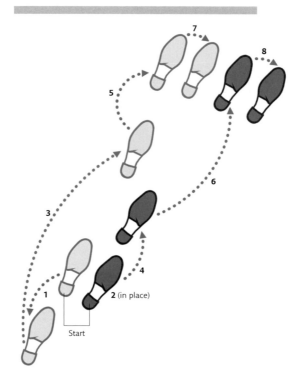

count:	**Man's Steps**

quick **1** Left foot takes a small step backwards.

quick **2** Right foot remains in place and the weight is taken onto it.

quick **3** Left foot takes a small step forwards, starting to draw your partner towards you.

a **4** Right foot closes towards left foot, still drawing partner towards you.

quick **5** Left foot takes a small step forwards, regaining normal hold.

quick **6** Right foot takes a small step to the side.

a **7** Left foot closes towards right foot.

quick **8** Right foot takes a small step to the side.

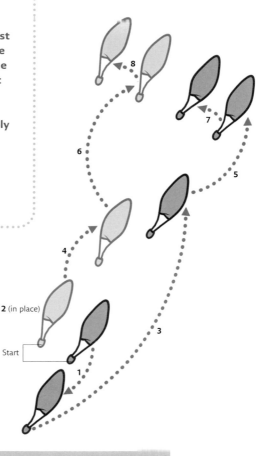

count:		**Lady's Steps**			
quick	**1**	**Right foot** takes a small step backwards.	quick	**5**	**Right foot** takes a small step forwards, regaining normal hold.
quick	**2**	**Left foot** remains in place and the weight is taken onto it.	quick	**6**	**Left foot** takes a small step to the side.
quick	**3**	**Right foot** takes a small step forwards, towards your partner.	a	**7**	**Right foot** closes towards left foot.
a	**4**	**Left foot** closes towards right foot.	quick	**8**	**Left foot** takes a small step to the side.

The Link in Jive Rhythm

1

count: quick

M **Left foot** takes a small step backwards.

L **Right foot** takes a small step backwards.

2

count: quick

M **Right foot** remains in place and weight is taken onto it.

L **Left foot** remains in place and weight is taken onto it.

5

count: quick

M **Left foot** takes a small step forwards, regaining normal hold.

L **Right foot** takes a small step forwards, regaining normal hold.

6

count: quick

M **Right foot** takes a small step to the side.

L **Left foot** takes a small step to the side.

3

count: quick

M Left foot takes a small step forwards, starting to draw your partner towards you.

L Right foot takes a small step forwards.

4

count: a

M Right foot closes towards left foot, still drawing your partner towards you.

L Left foot closes towards right foot.

7

count: a

M Left foot closes towards right foot.

L Right foot closes towards left foot.

8

count: quick

M Right foot takes a small step to the side.

L Left foot takes a small step to the side.

Jive Changes of Place, Right to Left

This figure precedes Jive Changes of Place, Left to Right (see pages 124–7). In the amalgamation of these two figures, the lady turns under the arch formed by the man's left and the lady's right joined hands. Each person moves away a little from their partner and then reverses the movement.

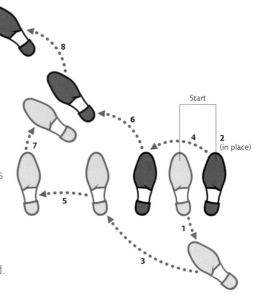

Man's Steps

count:

quick **1** Left foot backwards, turning to the left so that your left side moves further away from the lady's right side, making a small V shape.

quick **2** Right foot remains in place and weight is taken onto it, start turning the lady a little to her left with pressure from your right hand.

quick **3** Left foot takes a small step to the side, turning to your right and turning the lady to her left. She should now be nearly facing you.

a **4** Right foot closes a little way towards left foot, starting to raise your left and lady's right hand.

quick **5** Left foot takes a small step to the side, left hand raised, turning the lady to her right and guiding her by using a clockwise rotation of your left hand, which holds the lady's right hand loosely above her head.

quick **6** Right foot takes a small step to the side, turning to your left and finish the lady's strong turn to her right.

a **7** Left foot closes a little way towards the right foot.

quick **8** Right foot forwards, by now the lady will be facing you, drop the lady's right hand to waist level, still leaving your right hand free.

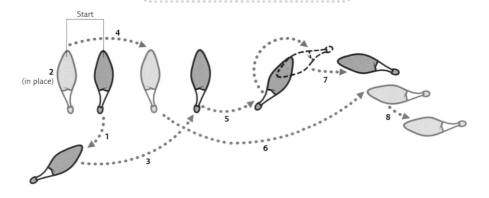

did you know?

Different rhythm

The Underarm Turn to Right for Lady on pages 112–13 shows this figure in Rock 'n' Roll style. It has four steps with the rhythm quick, quick, slow, slow, and the lady spins strongly to the right on step 3.

Lady's Steps

count:

quick 1 **Right foot** backwards, turning to the right so that your right side moves further away from the man's left side, making a small V shape.

quick 2 **Left foot** remains in place and weight is taken onto it, start turning a little to the left.

quick 3 **Right foot** takes a step to the side, turning left but with your right side still away from partner a little.

a 4 **Left foot** takes a small step towards the right foot.

quick 5 **Right foot** takes a small step to the side, starting a strong turn to the right.

quick 6 **Left foot** takes a small step to the side and backwards, completing the strong turn to the right.

a 7 **Right foot** takes a small step towards the left foot, still turning to the right.

quick 8 **Left foot** takes a small step to the side and backwards, you are now facing your partner.

Jive Changes of Place, Right to Left

1
count: quick

M **Left foot** takes a step backwards, turning to left, moving away from lady's right side.

L **Right foot** backwards, turning to right, moving away from man's left side.

2
count: quick

M **Right foot** remains in place, weight taken onto it, turning lady to her left.

L **Left foot** remains in place, weight taken onto it, turning a little to the left.

5
count: quick

M **Left foot** takes a small step to the side, turning lady to her right with left hand.

L **Right foot** takes a small step to the side, starting a strong turn to the right.

6
count: quick

M **Right foot** takes a small step to the side, completing the lady's turn to right.

L **Left foot** takes a small step to the side and backwards, completing strong turn to the right.

3
count: quick

M **Left foot** takes a small step to side, turning to your right and turning lady to her left.

L **Right foot** takes a step to the side, turning left but still away from partner.

4
count: a

M **Right foot** closes a little way towards left foot, starting to raise left and lady's right hand.

L **Left foot** takes a small step towards right foot.

7
count: a

M **Left foot** closes a little way towards right foot.

L **Right foot** takes a small step towards left foot, still turning to the right.

8
count: quick

M **Right foot** forwards, lady now facing you, still holding her right hand that can now drop to waist level.

L **Left foot** takes a small step to the side and backwards, now facing partner.

Jive Changes of Place, Left to Right

Follow the Jive Changes of Place, Right to Left (see pages 120–3) with this figure. The man leads the lady into her strong right turn by rotating her right hand clockwise with his left hand. While doing so he must not grip the lady's hand but allow it to rotate in his.

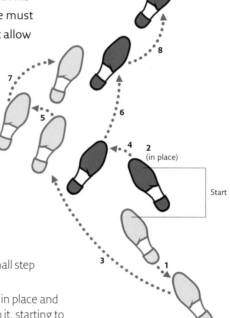

count:

Man's Steps

quick **1 Left foot** takes a small step backwards.

quick **2 Right foot** remains in place and weight is taken onto it, starting to turn a little to the right and to raise your left arm.

quick **3 Left foot** takes a step to the side, turning a little more to the right and continuing to raise your left arm so as to turn the lady to her left using an anti-clockwise rotation of your left hand.

a **4 Right foot** takes a small step towards left foot, still turning to the right and turning the lady to her left.

quick **5 Left foot** takes a step to the side, still turning to the right and turning the lady to her left.

quick **6 Right foot** takes a small step forwards, the lady now faces you.

a **7 Left foot** takes a small step towards right foot.

quick **8 Right foot** takes a small step forwards.

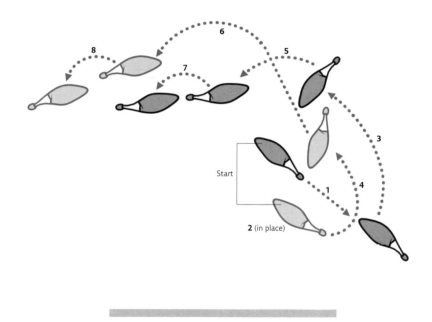

count: **Lady's Steps**

quick **1** **Right foot** takes a small step backwards.

quick **2** **Left foot** remains in place and weight is taken onto it, starting to turn to the left.

quick **3** **Right foot** takes a step to the side, turning to the left under the joined hands above your head.

a **4** **Left foot** closes a little way towards right foot, still turning to the left.

quick **5** **Right foot** takes a small step to the side, still turning to the left.

quick **6** **Left foot** takes a step backwards, you are now facing the man.

a **7** **Right foot** closes towards left foot.

quick **8** **Left foot** takes a small step backwards.

Jive Changes of Place, Left to Right

1

count: quick

M Left foot takes a small step backwards.

L Right foot takes a small step backwards.

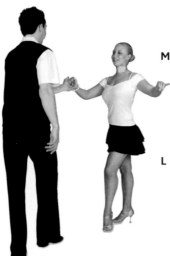

2

count: quick

M Right foot remains in place, weight is taken onto it, starting to turn to the right.

L Left foot remains in place, weight is taken onto it, starting to turn to the left.

5

count: quick

M Left foot takes a step to the side, still turning the lady to her left.

L Right foot takes a small step to the side, still turning to the left.

6

count: quick

M Right foot takes a small step forwards, the lady now faces you.

L Left foot takes a step backwards, you are now facing the man.

3

count: quick

M Left foot to the side, turning a little more to the right and continuing to turn the lady to her left.

L Right foot to the side, turning to the left under joined hands.

4

count: a

M Right foot takes a small step towards left foot, still turning the lady to her left.

L Left foot closes a little way towards right foot, still turning to the left.

7

count: a

M Left foot takes a small step towards right foot.

L Right foot closes towards left foot.

8

count: quick

M Right foot takes a small step forwards.

L Left foot takes a small step backwards.

6 Tango

In 1929, an important conference of dance teachers accepted the following as ballroom dances: Slow Foxtrot, Quickstep, Waltz, Tango and Blues. Tango now exists in two forms, the dance you will see in modern ballroom dance competitions and the Argentine Tango. The latter has a devoted following whose dance programme is exclusively that one dance. The ballroom Tango is unique as there is no rise and fall or lilt but it is danced flat with forward steps taken, as in walking, on the heel first. It should have a sultry feeling that some competition dancers lose if they become too aggressive.

Sultry and seductive

The Tango has a very special character all of its own. There
are erudite arguments about its true origins, and one French
academic claimed that he could trace it back to Ancient Greece.

Generally, the Tango is believed to have originated in Argentina,
and especially Buenos Aires. In the early years of the 20th century
it was danced solo by prostitutes to entice men into the bordellos.
It developed into a dance for couples with, at its more advanced
levels, intricate movements where partners' legs became
intertwined and with very close body contact. This became
known as the Argentine Tango. Ballroom Tango, which is
taught here, shares the same origins, but it is the one seen
danced in competitions.

Staccato rhythm

As with all dances, Tango has changed over the years. The basic
rhythm of the music has changed from that of the Habanera to
Milonga. In the mid-1930s a German dancer, Freddie Camp,
revolutionized the dance with a more vigorous approach to the
rhythm that has become known as staccato. In recent years, this
has been somewhat overdone but does not affect those learning
the dance at the early stages.

The character of the dance is unique. It does not flow in the
same way as most body-contact dances with each step blending
into the next and with a flow of body movement. In Tango
each step is taken much as in walking. There are three major
differences. One: the hold is much more compact and the man
reaches further around his partner with his right hand and arm.
Two: the feet are picked up and placed into position rather than
skimming the floor. Three: the pattern of walking steps follows a
slight curve to the left so that when the man steps forwards with

A poster advertising
a 1913 silent film
featuring Max Linder.
Many regard Linder
as a more important
early comedian than
Charlie Chaplin. The
poster illustrates
the popularity of the
Tango when the film
was released.

his left foot the step is taken slightly across the body. If dancers keep in mind the movement of any member of the cat family when stalking prey, that will go a long way to achieving the correct character for the dance.

In many ways the Tango is an easy dance, but to achieve feeling for the dance the music is vital. It is important to listen to the music, the tune as well as the rhythm. The music is in 2/4 and has a more authentic feeling when it is in a minor key.

A couple clearly enjoying the Tango and dancing in promenade position, where the man's left and the lady's right side move away from one another – body contact is retained at hip level.

Basic Tango hold

The couple stand in very close contact, with the lady's right hip roughly central on the man's body. The man reaches further around the lady with his right hand and arm, and his left hand is drawn closer to the head than in the other ballroom dances. The lady moves her left hand further around the man's right arm.

The Walks into the Progressive Side Step

In this figure steps 1–2 are known as the Walks and steps 3–6 are the Progressive Side Step. The complete figure makes a slight curve to the left.

count:

Man's Steps

Start facing the nearest wall, then twist your body a little to the left bringing your right shoulder forwards.

slow **1** **Left foot** takes a step forwards and slightly across the line of the right foot, with the left foot turned very slightly out, that is, pointing a little to the left, taking one beat of music.

slow **2** **Right foot** takes a step forwards with the foot pointing a little to the left, taking one beat of music.

quick **3** **Left foot** takes a step forwards and slightly across the line of the right foot with the left foot turned very slightly out, that is, pointing a little to the left, taking half a beat of music.

quick **4** **Right foot** takes a small step to the side and slightly back of left foot, taking half a beat of music.

slow **5** **Left foot** takes a step forwards and slightly across the line of the right foot with the left foot turned very slightly out, that is, pointing a little to the left, taking one beat of music.

slow **6** **Right foot** takes a step forwards with the foot pointing a little to the left, taking one beat of music.

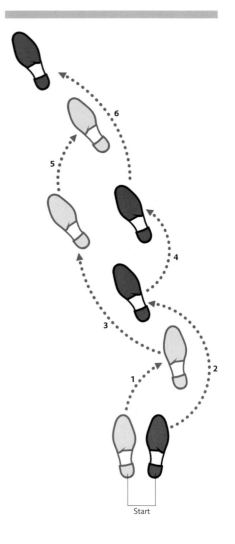

Start

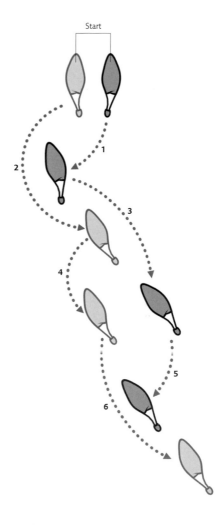

count: **Lady's Steps**

Start backing the nearest wall, then twist your body a little to the left bringing your left shoulder backwards.

slow **1 Right foot** takes a step backwards and slightly across the line of the left foot, with the right foot turned in very slightly, that is, pointing a little to the left, taking one beat of music.

slow **2 Left foot** takes a step backwards with the foot pointing a little to the left, taking one beat of music.

quick **3 Right foot** takes a step backwards and slightly across the line of the left foot with the right foot turned very slightly in, that is, pointing a little to the left, taking half a beat of music.

quick **4 Left foot** takes a small step to the side and slightly forwards of right foot, with foot pointing a little to the left, taking half a beat of music.

slow **5 Right foot** takes a step backwards and slightly across the line of the left foot, with the right foot turned very slightly in, that is, pointing a little to the left, taking one beat of music.

slow **6 Left foot** takes a step backwards, with the foot pointing a little to the left, taking one beat of music.

The Walks into the Progressive Side Step

1

count: slow

M Left foot forwards and slightly across the line of the right foot.

L Right foot backwards and slightly across the line of the left foot.

Takes one beat of music.

2

count: slow

M Right foot forwards with the foot pointing a little to the left.

L Left foot backwards with foot pointing a little to the left.

Takes one beat of music.

4

count: quick

M Right foot a small step to the side and slightly back of left foot.

L Left foot to the side and slightly forwards of right foot.

Takes half a beat of music.

5

count: slow

M Left foot forwards and slightly across the line of the right foot.

L Right foot backwards and slightly across the line of the left foot.

Takes one beat of music.

3

count: quick

M Left foot forwards and across the line of the right foot.

L Right foot backwards and slightly across the line of the left foot.

Takes half a beat of music.

6

count: slow

M Right foot forwards with the foot pointing a little to the left.

L Left foot backwards with foot pointing a little to the left.

Takes one beat of music.

must know

Walking pattern
Part of the special Tango atmosphere arises from the walking pattern. If a consecutive number of forward steps are taken, the path the walks follow should curve quite strongly to the left. This curve creates the desirable right shoulder lead.

Progressive Link into Promenade

This figure can follow The Walks into the Progressive Side Step (see pages 132–5), either after step 2 or step 6, and is used when you want to turn into promenade position. This position is reached by the use of the Progressive Link (steps 1–2).

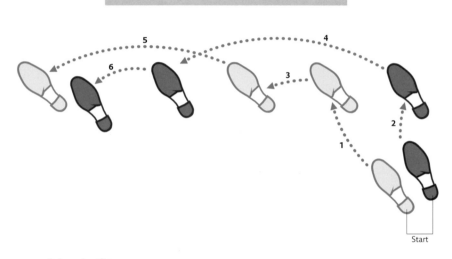

Start

count: Man's Steps

Start by 'facing diagonally to wall' in normal close Tango hold. By step 2 you should be 'facing diagonally to wall' in promenade position.

quick **1** Left foot takes a step forwards and slightly across the line of the right foot with the left foot pointing a little to the left.

quick **2** Right foot takes a small step to the side and slightly behind the line of left foot. Press firmly on the lady's back with heel of right hand to guide her to turn into promenade position.

slow **3** Left foot takes a step to the side along a line parallel to the wall in promenade position, with left foot pointing diagonally to wall.

quick **4** Right foot steps across left foot, moving foot along a line parallel to the wall, still in promenade position, with foot pointing diagonally to wall.

quick **5** Left foot takes a step to the side along a line parallel to the wall, with left foot pointing diagonally to wall, and turning partner to face you.

slow **6** Right foot closes to left foot, closing right toe to left instep.

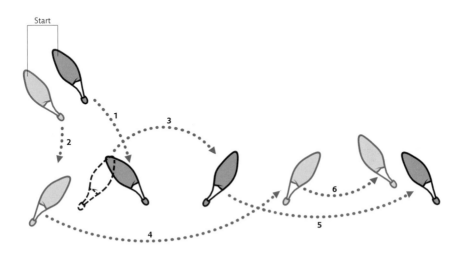

Start

1

2

3

4

5

6

count: **Lady's Steps**

Start by 'backing diagonally to wall' in normal close Tango hold. By step 2 you should be 'facing diagonally to centre' in promenade position.

quick **1 Right foot** takes a step backwards and slightly across the line of the left foot with the right foot pointing a little to the left.

quick **2 Left foot** takes a small step to side and slightly behind the line of right foot, turning to the right into promenade position with right side 25 cm (1 ft) or so away from partner.

slow **3 Right foot** takes a step to the side along a line parallel to the wall in promenade position, with right foot pointing diagonally to centre.

quick **4 Left foot** steps across right foot, moving foot along a line parallel to the wall, in promenade position, with left foot pointing diagonally to centre.

quick **5 Right foot** takes a step to the side along a line parallel to the wall, turning to the left to face the man and 'backing diagonally to wall'.

slow **6 Left foot** closes to right foot, closing left instep to right toe.

Progressive Link into Promenade

1
count: quick

M Left foot forwards and slightly across line of right foot.

L Right foot backwards and slightly across line of left foot.

2
count: quick

M Right foot takes a small step to the side behind line of left foot, pressing firmly on lady's back with right hand.

L Left foot takes a small step to side and turning into promenade position.

5
count: quick

M Left foot to side along a line parallel to the wall, turning lady to face you.

L Right foot to side along a line parallel to the wall, turning to the left to face partner.

6
count: slow

M Right foot closes to left foot, closing right toe to left instep.

L Left foot closes to right foot, closing left instep to right toe. This is the Tango closed position.

3

count: slow

M Left foot takes a step to the side along a line parallel to the wall in promenade position.

L Right foot takes a step to the side along a line parallel to the wall, in promenade position.

4

count: quick

M Right foot steps across left foot along a line parallel to the wall.

L Left foot steps across right foot along a line parallel to the wall.

Open Promenade

While similar to the Promenade, this figure has a different form of ending. Like the Promenade you need to be in the promenade position, using the Progressive Link (see pages 136–9) to start. The figure can be followed by The Walks (see pages 132–5), with partners coming in line with one another on the first step, that is, with the man's left foot following the line of the lady's right foot. Alternatively, dance the Rock on Left Foot (see pages 144–7) after this figure.

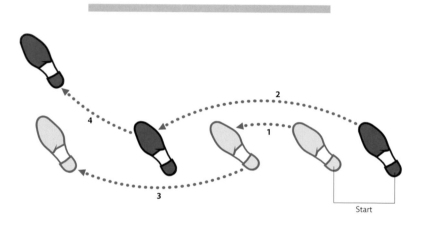

Man's Steps

count:

slow **1** Left foot takes a step to the side along a line parallel to the wall in promenade position, with the left foot pointing diagonally to wall.

quick **2** Right foot steps across left foot moving the foot along a line parallel to wall, still in promenade position with right foot pointing diagonally to wall.

quick **3** Left foot takes a step to the side along a line parallel to the wall, with left foot pointing diagonally to wall, and turning your partner to face you.

slow **4** Right foot takes a step forwards across your body passing to your left of your partner's body – 'outside partner'. Try to maintain body contact throughout the step.

must know

Lady must turn
On all Promenade figures in Tango, the man should make sure that the turn away from partner is made by the lady. He should resist turning his left side away from his partner. The lady must do all the necessary turning, both away from and back to face the man.

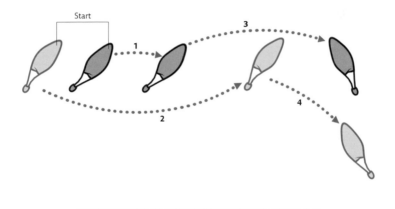

count: **Lady's Steps**

slow **1 Right foot** takes a step to the side along a line parallel to the wall, in promenade position, with the right foot pointing diagonally to centre.

quick **2 Left foot** steps across right foot moving foot along a line parallel to wall, in promenade position, with left foot pointing diagonally to centre.

quick **3 Right foot** takes a step to the side along a line parallel to the wall, turning to the left to face your partner.

slow **4 Left foot** takes a step backwards, with partner stepping to the right side of your body. Try to maintain body contact as the step is taken.

Open Promenade

1
count: slow

M **Left foot** takes a step to the side along a line parallel to the wall.

L **Right foot** takes a step to the side along a line parallel to the wall.

2
count: quick

M **Right foot** steps across left foot along a line parallel to the wall.

L **Left foot** steps across right foot along a line parallel to the wall.

3
count: quick

M **Left foot** takes a step to the side along a line parallel to the wall, turning lady to face you.

L **Right foot** takes a step to the side along a line parallel to the wall, turning to the left to face partner.

4
count: slow

M **Right foot** steps forwards across your body stepping 'outside partner'.

L **Left foot** steps backwards with partner stepping to your right.

Rock on Left Foot (with Closed Ending)

On the first three steps of this group the couple do not move their feet, but as the name suggests, merely rock their weight backwards and forwards from foot to foot. This figure should be danced after the Open Promenade (see pages 140–3).

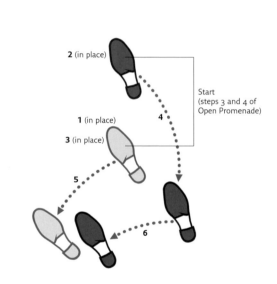

2 (in place)

Start
(steps 3 and 4 of
Open Promenade)

1 (in place)

4

3 (in place)

5

6

Man's Steps

count:

quick **1** **Transfer weight** backwards onto left foot with partner on your right side.

quick **2** **Transfer weight** forwards onto right foot with partner still on your right side.

slow **3** **Transfer weight** backwards onto left foot with partner still on your right side.

quick **4** **Right foot** takes a step backwards, beginning to turn to left and bringing partner into line so that her left foot follows the line of your right foot.

quick **5** **Left foot** takes a small step to the side, still turning to the left.

slow **6** **Right foot** closes to left foot with right toe closing to left instep (the typical Tango closed position).

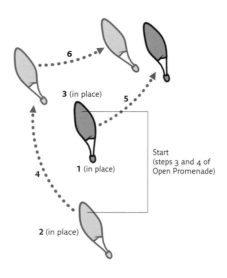

6

3 (in place)

5

1 (in place)

Start
(steps 3 and 4 of
Open Promenade)

4

2 (in place)

count: ## Lady's Steps

quick **1** Transfer weight forwards onto right foot with partner on your right side.

quick **2** Transfer weight backwards onto left foot with partner still on your right side.

slow **3** Transfer weight forwards onto right foot with partner still on your right side.

quick **4** Left foot takes a step forwards, beginning to turn to left and moving into line with partner.

quick **5** Right foot takes a step to the side, still turning to the left.

slow **6** Left foot closes to right foot with left instep closing to right toe (the typical Tango closed position).

Rock on Left Foot (with Closed Ending)

1

count: quick

M Transfer weight backwards onto left foot, lady on your right side.

L Transfer weight forwards onto right foot, with the man on your right side.

2

count: quick

M Transfer weight forwards onto right foot, lady still on right side.

L Transfer weight backwards onto left foot, with the man still on your right side.

4

count: quick

M Right foot backwards, beginning to turn to the left.

L Left foot forwards, beginning to turn to the left and moving into line with partner.

5

count: quick

M Left foot takes a small step to the side, still turning to the left.

L Right foot takes a small step to the side, still turning to the left.

3

count: slow

M Transfer weight backwards onto left foot, lady still on right side.

L Transfer weight forwards onto right foot, with the man still on your right side.

6

count: slow

M Right foot closes to left foot with right toe closing to left instep.

L Left foot closes to right foot with left instep closing to right toe.

want to know more?

• For advice on choosing a dance studio see page 183.
• If you decide to join a dance school, see the studios listed on pages 184–9. If there is no local school listed, the Dance Teacher Associations on pages 183–4 will be happy to let you have details of their members in your area.
• Read *Tango: An Art History of Love* by Robert Farris Thompson.
• Watch the film *Assassination Tango*, which captures the power of the dance.

weblinks

• Learn more about the history of the Tango at: en.wikipedia.org /wiki/Tango (or wiki /Argentine_Tango for the South American dance).
• For specialist dancewear, go to Chrisanne Ltd at: www.chrisanne.co.uk

7 Slow Foxtrot

This is an especially British dance. It was
born in the late 1920s and, despite being a
little more difficult than other dances, is the
favourite dance of most skilled dancers. It is
a dance that should flow and is at its best
when 'fancy' figures are eschewed. However,
do not let any additional difficulty put you
off – the dance will charm you not as a
spectator but when you experience it.

International style

All dancers are likely to have a preference for a particular dance. The dance you are about to learn is the favourite dance of most, if not all, good dancers.

The Slow Foxtrot is a dance that relies on the continuous movement and flow of the dancing couple for its enjoyment. Its roots go back to the years following World War I (post 1918). The early pioneers were exploring the possibilities of new styles of dance that did not rely on prescribed sequences. With the exception of the Waltz, previously popular dance functions, balls or assemblies had comprised dances based on arranged patterns of dance steps to specially arranged music. For instance, the Veleta, devised by Arthur Morris of Leeds, and the Military Two Step, devised by James Finnigan (who was the Master of Ceremonies at the Empress Ballroom, Blackpool, where the British Dance Championships are and have been held for many years).

Departing from tradition

Up until this time all ballroom dances had been based on the five positions of the feet established in the world of ballet in the 17th century by Pierre Beauchamps for the French Court. For popular dance to depart from such a long-established tradition was revolutionary. There were many new dance forms as a result, but the British Slow Foxtrot became accepted worldwide and is often called International Style. The dance was developed by British dancers such as Josephine Bradley, dancing with American amateur dancer Wellesley Smith, Victor and Dolly Silvester, and many more.

Its beauty relies not on intricate footwork but on the rolling flow that can be created. The dance is truly joyful and is really

only fully appreciated by those dancing. It is not a particularly good vehicle for exhibition dancing. It relies on good body stance for both man and lady and, since the man has to guide his partner into the various dance figures, good body contact is essential. This unison between the couple is itself one of the pleasures of the dance.

In the Slow Foxtrot, steps taken forwards or sideways and counted 'quick' are usually taken on the ball of the foot.

The count and music

All the figures explained in this section consist of a combination of slow and quick steps. The music is in 4/4 time, quick steps take one beat of the music and slow steps two. Normally throughout the Slow Foxtrot all steps taken forwards and counted slow will be taken leading with the heel of the foot, rather like walking, but swinging the leg more from the hip than moving it from the knee. Steps taken forwards or sideways and counted 'quick' will usually be taken on the ball of the foot.

Walk and Feather Step to Three Step

This easy-to-follow introductory group is intended to get you used to the flow of the dance. Steps 2–7 inclusive can be repeated as often as desired. If you approach a corner, steps 5–7 inclusive can be curved to the left a quarter of a full turn (90 degrees) so as to move along the next side of the room.

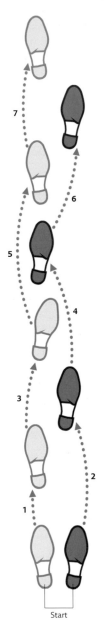

Man's Steps

count:

Start with your right shoulder pointing to the nearest wall so you are looking along the room.

slow   **1 Left foot** takes a step forwards.

slow   **2 Right foot** takes a step forwards, turning body slightly to the right.

quick   **3 Left foot** takes a step forwards, leading with the left side of the body.

quick   **4 Right foot** takes a step forwards to your left of your partner ('outside partner').

slow   **5 Left foot** takes a step forwards in line with partner.

quick   **6 Right foot** takes a step forwards, a little longer than is normal for 'quick' steps and, unusually, taken on the heel first.

quick   **7 Left foot** takes a step forwards, as is usual for steps with quick timing, on the ball of the foot.

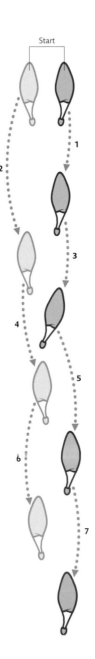

count: **Lady's Steps**

slow **1 Right foot** takes a step backwards.

slow **2 Left foot** takes a step backwards, turning body slightly to the right.

quick **3 Right foot** takes a step backwards, leading with the right side of the body.

quick **4 Left foot** takes a step backwards, with partner stepping to your right ('outside partner').

slow **5 Right foot** takes a step backwards in line with partner.

quick **6 Left foot** takes a step backwards, a little longer than is normal for 'quick' steps.

quick **7 Right foot** takes a step backwards.

Walk and Feather Step to Three Step

1

count: slow

M Left foot takes a step forwards.

L Right foot takes a step backwards.

2

count: slow

M Right foot takes a step forwards, turning the body slightly to the right.

L Left foot takes a step backwards, turning the body slightly to the right.

5

count: slow

M Left foot takes a step forwards in line with partner.

L Right foot takes a step backwards in line with partner.

6

count: quick

M Right foot takes a step forwards, a little longer than is normal for 'quick' steps and, unusually, taken on the heel first.

L Left foot takes a step backwards, a little longer than is normal for 'quick' steps.

3

count: quick

M   **Left foot** takes a step forwards, leading with the left side of the body.

L   **Right foot** takes a step backwards, leading with the right side of the body.

4

count: quick

M   **Right foot** takes a step forwards to your left of your partner.

L   **Left foot** takes a step backwards, with partner stepping to your right ('outside partner').

7

count: quick

M   **Left foot** takes a step forwards, as is usual for steps with quick timing, on the ball of the foot.

L   **Right foot** takes a step backwards.

Walk and Feather Step to Open Reverse Turn and Change of Direction

This amalgamation of three figures will get you moving in the Slow Foxtrot and introduces turns. Step 1 is the Walk, steps 2, 3 and 4 are the Feather Step, steps 5–10 inclusive are the Open Reverse Turn, and steps 11–14 are the Change of Direction.

count:

Man's Steps

Start by standing with your right shoulder pointing to the nearest wall and then turn 45 degrees to your left so that you are facing into the room in a slanting direction. Dancers call this 'facing diagonally to centre'.

slow **1** **Left foot** takes a step forwards.

slow **2** **Right foot** takes a step forwards, turning body slightly to the right.

quick **3** **Left foot** takes a step forwards, leading with the left side of the body.

quick **4** **Right foot** takes a step forwards, stepping to your left of your partner's feet ('outside partner').

slow **5** **Left foot** takes a step forwards, beginning to turn to the left.

quick **6** **Right foot** takes a step to the side, still turning to left. By now you should have turned so that you are backing slanting out of the room – you should have turned 90 degrees from the start of the figure – now 'backing diagonally to wall'.

quick **7** **Left foot** takes a step backwards along a line parallel to the nearest wall, still turning to the left with partner stepping to the right of your feet ('partner outside').

slow **8** **Right foot** takes a step backwards turning to the left, the lady's left foot is now in line with your right foot.

quick **9** **Left foot** takes a step to the side, still turning to the left – your left foot is now pointing diagonally to the nearest wall.

quick **10** **Right foot** takes a step forwards to your left of your partner's feet ('outside partner').

slow **11** **Left foot** takes a step forwards, turning to the left in line with partner.

quick **12** **Right foot** takes a step diagonally forwards on the inside edge of flat foot, still turning to the left and leading with the right shoulder. To help you control the figure, bend your knees slightly.

quick **13** **Left foot** closes to right foot, drawing the foot along the floor, closing left instep to right toe and retaining weight of the body on the right foot, by now you should be 'facing diagonally to centre'.

slow **14** **Left foot** takes a step forwards.

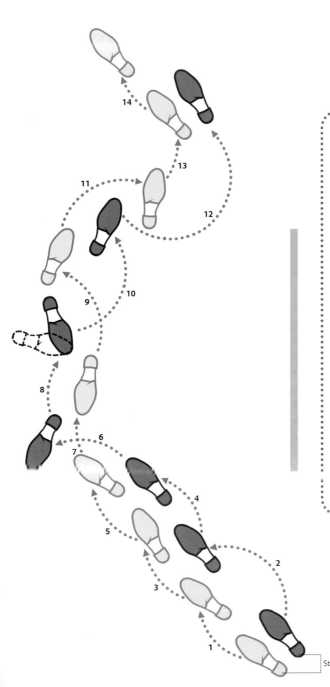

must know

Cornering

When approaching a corner, make an additional turn over steps 11–13, making a total of half a full turn over these steps to leave the man facing diagonally to centre in respect of the new wall along which the dance will progress. During the Change of Direction – especially on steps 11 and 12 – both partners should bend their knees slightly. On step 13, when the man closes his left foot to his right foot, and when the lady closes her right foot to her left foot, the ball of the moving foot should be pressed against the floor to control the momentum.

Start

Walk and Feather Step to Open Reverse Turn and Change of Direction (continued)

count: **Lady's Steps**

Start by standing with your left shoulder pointing to the nearest wall and then turn 45 degrees to your left so that you are facing out of the room in a slanting direction. Dancers call this 'backing diagonally to centre'.

slow **1 Right foot** takes a step backwards.

slow **2 Left foot** takes a step backwards.

quick **3 Right foot** takes a step backwards, turning body slightly to the right.

quick **4 Left foot** takes a step backwards, with partner stepping to your right of your feet ('partner outside').

slow **5 Right foot** takes a step backwards, beginning to turn to left.

quick **6 Left foot** takes a step to the side, still turning to the left, by now you should have turned so that you are facing slanting out of the room, 'facing diagonally to wall'. You should have turned 90 degrees from the start of the figure.

quick **7 Right foot** takes a step forwards along a line parallel to the nearest wall, still turning to the left and stepping to the left of your partner's feet ('outside partner').

slow **8 Left foot** takes a step forwards, turning to the left, your left foot is now in line with partner's right foot.

quick **9 Right foot** takes a step to the side, still turning to the left.

quick **10 Left foot** takes a step backwards, with partner stepping to the right of your feet ('partner outside').

slow **11 Right foot** takes a step backwards, partner in line, turning to the left.

quick **12 Left foot** takes a step diagonally backwards, still turning to the left. Although this is a quick step, do not rise to the balls of the feet as would normally be the case.

quick **13 Right foot** closes to left foot, drawing the foot along the floor closing right toes to left instep and retaining the weight of the body on the left foot.

slow **14 Right foot** takes a step backwards.

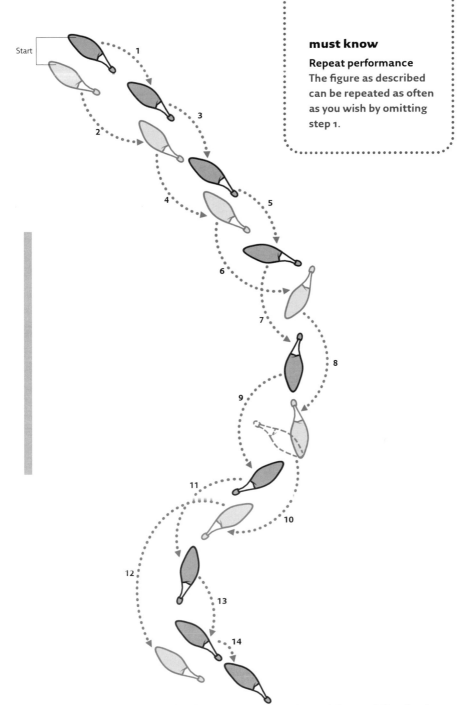

Start

must know

Repeat performance
The figure as described can be repeated as often as you wish by omitting step 1.

1
2
3
4
5
6
7
8
9
10
11
12
13
14

Walk and Feather Step to Open Reverse Turn and Change of Direction

1

count: slow

M Left foot takes a step forwards.

L Right foot takes a step backwards.

2

count: slow

M Right foot takes a step forwards, turning your body slightly to the right.

L Left foot takes a step backwards.

5

count: slow

M Left foot takes a step forwards, beginning to turn to the left.

L Right foot takes a step backwards, beginning to turn to the left.

6

count: quick

M Right foot takes a step to the side, still turning to the left. By now you should have turned so that you are 'backing diagonally to wall'.

L Left foot takes a step to the side, still turning to the left, by now you should have turned so that you are 'facing diagonally to wall'.

3

count: quick

M Left foot takes a step forwards, leading with the left side of the body.

L Right foot takes a step backwards, turning your body slightly to the right.

4

count: quick

M Right foot takes a step forwards, stepping to your left of your partner's feet ('outside partner').

L Left foot takes a step backwards, with partner stepping to your right of your feet ('partner outside').

7

count: quick

M Left foot takes a step backwards along a line parallel to the nearest wall, still turning to the left with partner stepping to the right of your feet.

L Right foot takes a step forwards along a line parallel to the nearest wall, still turning to the left and stepping left of your partner's feet.

8

count: slow

M Right foot takes a step backwards turning to the left, the lady's left foot is now in line with your right foot.

L Left foot takes a step forwards, turning to the left, your left foot is now in line with partner's right foot.

(continued overleaf)

Walk and Feather Step to Open Reverse Turn and Change of Direction (continued)

9

count: quick

M Left foot takes a step to the side, still turning to the left – your left foot is now pointing diagonally to the nearest wall.

L Right foot takes a step to the side, still turning to the left.

10

count: quick

M Right foot takes a step forwards to your left of your partner's feet ('outside partner').

L Left foot takes a step backwards, with partner stepping to the right of your feet ('partner outside').

12

count: quick

M Right foot takes a step diagonally forwards on the inside edge of flat foot, still turning to the left and leading with right shoulder.

L Left foot takes a step diagonally backwards, still turning to the left. Do not rise to the balls of the feet as you would normally with a quick step.

13

count: quick

M Left foot closes to right foot, drawing the foot along the floor, closing left instep to right toes (weight on right foot).

L Right foot closes to left foot, drawing the foot along the floor, closing right toes to left instep (weight on left foot).

11

count: slow

M Left foot takes a step forwards in line with partner, turning to the left.

L Right foot takes a step backwards, partner in line, turning to the left.

14

count: slow

M Left foot takes a step forwards.

L Right foot takes a step backwards.

> **must know**
>
> **Perfect posture**
> A good carriage of the body is essential in Slow Foxtrot. Both man and lady should stand erect but avoid lifting or tensing the shoulders. The man should avoid a rigid appearance, while the trunk of the lady's body will lean backwards slightly from the waist up, but keep this relaxed and do not overdo it.

The Heel Turn

This is not a dance figure but a turning action that is helpful at this stage. In the Open Telemark (see pages 166–73) and on many other figures the lady has to make a 'heel turn'. A mark of a female dancer's ability is how well she can perform this technique.

On occasions the man also has to be able to dance a heel turn but his are less frequent and mostly done starting on his left foot. The heel turn here for the lady is on her right foot but the man can also try it by substituting 'left' for 'right' and so on in the exercise to follow. When the lady is comfortable doing a heel turn starting with the right foot she should then try it starting on the left foot and turning to the right.

The exercise involves going through the foot positions of the heel turn but without turn and stressing the correct use of foot and ankle muscles as the foot moves back to position. When you are comfortable with the pattern try adding a little turn as the left foot closes to the right foot. Start with just a little turn, say about 45 degrees, and then when you are comfortable increase it first to 90 degrees and then eventually to 135 degrees.

No turn   **45° turn**   **135° turn**

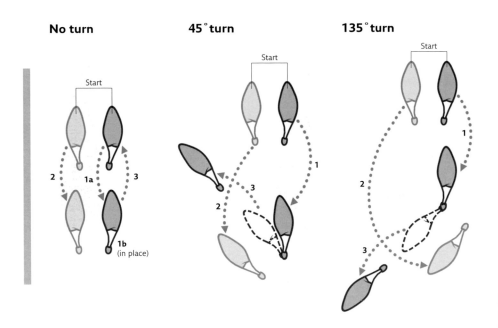

Step 1a

Standing with the feet together and with the body weight over the left foot, move the right foot backwards, swinging the leg from the hip. The right leg should be straight but not stiff, with the ankle and toes stretched backwards. Try to straighten the ankle so that anyone standing behind you can see the sole of your shoe.

Step 1b

When you reach a comfortable position, start to move the body weight from the front (left) foot to the right foot, allowing the right foot to compress and lowering the heel towards the floor. The right foot acts like a spring controlling the transfer of weight from the front to the back foot.

Step 2

Continue moving the weight of the body backwards onto the right foot, and at the same time draw the left foot back towards it. Close the left foot to the right foot and transfer the full weight of the body onto it.

Step 3

Moving the right leg from the hip, the right foot takes a short step forwards on the ball of the foot.

Walk and Feather Step to Open Telemark, Feather Ending and Change of Direction

Man's Steps

count:

Start by facing down the room with your right shoulder pointing towards the nearest wall and then turn 45 degrees to your left to finish facing slanting into the room – 'facing diagonally to centre'.

slow **1 Left foot** takes a step forwards.

slow **2 Right foot** takes a step forwards, turning the body slightly to the right.

quick **3 Left foot** takes a step forwards leading with the left side of the body.

quick **4 Right foot** takes a step forwards to your left of your partner's feet ('outside partner').

slow **5 Left foot** takes a step forwards turning to the left.

quick **6 Right foot** takes a step sideways on the same line as the left foot, still turning to the left. Try to avoid pulling the lady to her left so that it is not difficult for her to close her feet.

quick **7 Left foot** takes a step sideways along an imaginary line diagonal to the nearest wall, still turning to the left. At the same time guide the lady to turn her right side away from you into promenade position – the guide should come from increasing the pressure on the lady's back with the heel of your right hand and not by pushing your left hand forwards.

slow **8 Right foot** takes a step forwards diagonally to the nearest wall in promenade position and starting to turn your partner to face towards you again.

quick **9 Left foot** takes a step forwards diagonally to nearest wall, partner turning to face you.

quick **10 Right foot** takes a step forwards to your left of your partner's feet ('outside partner').

slow **11 Left foot** takes a step forwards in line with partner, turning to the left.

quick **12 Right foot** takes a step diagonally forwards on the inside edge of flat foot, still turning to the left and leading with the right shoulder. It will help control the figure if you bend your knees slightly.

quick **13 Left foot** closes to right foot, drawing the foot along the floor, closing left instep to right toes, and retaining weight of the body on the right foot. By now you should be 'facing diagonally to centre'.

slow **14 Left foot** takes a step forwards.

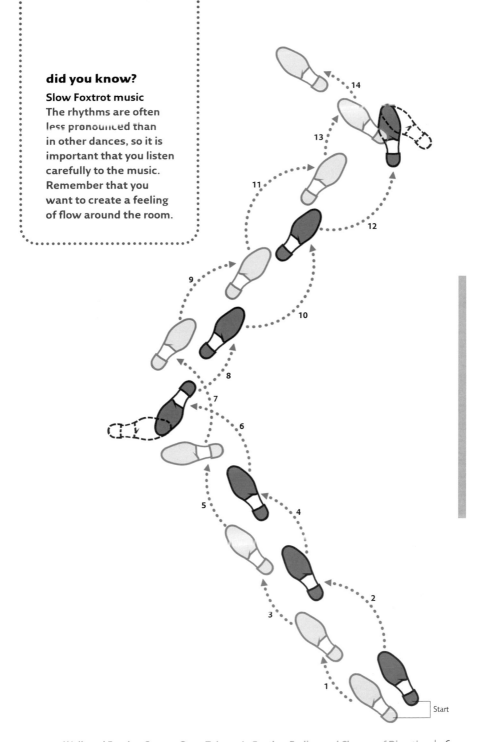

Slow Foxtrot music
The rhythms are often less pronounced than in other dances, so it is important that you listen carefully to the music. Remember that you want to create a feeling of flow around the room.

Walk and Feather Step to Open Telemark, Feather Ending and Change of Direction (continued)

count:

Lady's Steps

Start by standing with your left shoulder pointing to the nearest wall and then turn 45 degrees to your left so that you are facing out of the room in a slanting direction. Dancers call this 'backing diagonally to centre'.

slow **1** Right foot takes a step backwards.

slow **2** Left foot takes a step backwards, turning the body slightly to the right.

quick **3** Right foot takes a step backwards, leading with the right side of the body.

quick **4** Left foot takes a step backwards, with partner stepping to your right ('partner outside').

slow **5** Right foot takes a step backwards, turning to the left. This is the first step of a Heel Turn.

quick **6** Left foot closes to right foot, still turning left into heel turn.

quick **7** Right foot takes a step diagonally forwards in promenade position, that is, with your right side further away from your partner than your left side.

slow **8** Left foot takes a step forwards and across in promenade position, that is, through the space between your right and your partner's left foot, starting to turn to left to face towards him.

quick **9** Right foot takes a step to the side, turning to the left to face partner.

quick **10** Left foot takes a step backwards, with partner stepping to the right of your feet ('outside partner').

slow **11** Right foot takes a step backwards turning to the left, partner in line.

quick **12** Left foot takes a step diagonally backwards, still turning to the left. Although this is a quick step, do not rise to the balls of the feet as would normally be the case. It will help control the figure if you bend your knees slightly.

quick **13** Right foot closes to left foot, drawing the foot along the floor, closing right toes to left instep, and retaining the weight of the body on the left foot.

slow **14** Right foot takes a step backwards.

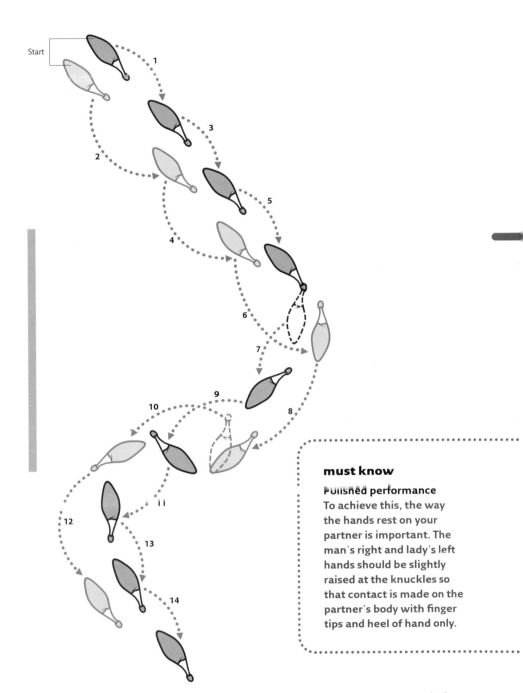

Start

1

2

3

4

5

6

7

8

9

10

11

12

13

14

Walk and Feather Step to Open Telemark, Feather Ending and Change of Direction

1

count: slow

M Left foot takes a step forwards.

L Right foot takes a step backwards.

2

count: slow

M Right foot takes a step forwards, turning the body slightly to the right.

L Left foot takes a step backwards, turning the body slightly to the right.

5

count: slow

M Left foot takes a step forwards turning to the left.

L Right foot takes a step backwards, turning to the left. This is the first step of a Heel Turn.

6

count: quick

M Right foot takes a step sideways on the same line as the left foot, still turning to the left. Try to avoid pulling the lady to her left so as to avoid making it difficult for her to close her feet.

L Left foot closes to right foot, still turning left into heel turn.

3

count: quick

M **Left foot** takes a step forwards leading with the left side of the body.

L **Right foot** takes a step backwards, leading with the right side of the body.

4

count: quick

M **Right foot** takes a step forwards to your left of your partner's feet ('outside partner').

L **Left foot** takes a step backwards, with partner stepping to your right ('partner outside').

7

count: quick

M **Left foot** takes a step sideways along an imaginary line diagonal to the nearest wall, still turning to the left. At the same time, guide the lady to turn her right side away from you into promenade position.

L **Right foot** takes a step diagonally forwards in promenade position.

8

count: slow

M **Right foot** takes a step forwards diagonally to the nearest wall in promenade position, starting to turn your partner to face you.

L **Left foot** takes a step forwards and across, through the space between your right and your partner's left foot.

(continued overleaf)

Walk and Feather Step to Open Telemark, Feather Ending and Change of Direction (continued)

9

count: quick

M Left foot takes a step forwards diagonally to nearest wall, partner turning to face you.

L Right foot takes a step to the side, turning to the left to face partner.

10

count: quick

M Right foot takes a step forwards to your left of your partner's feet ('outside partner').

L Left foot takes a step backwards, with partner stepping to the right of your feet ('outside partner').

12

count: quick

M Right foot takes a step diagonally forwards on the inside edge of flat foot, still turning to the left and leading with right shoulder.

L Left foot takes a step diagonally backwards, still turning to the left. Do not rise to the balls of the feet as you would normally for a quick step.

13

count: quick

M Left foot closes to right foot, drawing the foot along the floor, closing left instep to right toes (weight on right foot). By now you should be 'facing diagonally to centre'.

L Right foot closes to left foot, drawing the foot along the floor, closing right toes to left instep (weight on left foot).

11

count: slow

M **Left foot** takes a step forwards, turning to the left in line with partner.

L **Right foot** takes a step backwards, turning to the left, partner in line.

14

count: slow

M **Left foot** takes a step forwards

L **Right foot** takes a step backwards.

must know

Practise balance
To help improve your footwork do this simple exercise. Stand with feet together, rise to the toes and then lower back to the floor. Repeat this several times both quickly and slowly. When on the toes, hold for a few seconds, this will improve your balance.

Walk and Curving Feather Step to Reverse Wave

This figure introduces the concept of the man moving backwards and carrying the lady with him. Normally the man generates the 'power' for figures, but here the lady has the responsibility of providing the forwards momentum for the steps when she is moving forwards and the man is moving backwards.

count:

Man's Steps

Start with your right shoulder pointing towards the nearest wall and then turn 45 degrees to your left to finish facing slanting into the room – 'facing diagonally to centre'.

slow **1** **Left foot** takes a step forwards.

slow **2** **Right foot** takes a step forwards, turning slightly to the right.

quick **3** **Left foot** takes a step forwards, still turning to the right.

quick **4** **Right foot** takes a step forwards, stepping to your left of your partner's feet ('outside partner'). By now you should have turned to be facing the line of dance, that is, with your right shoulder pointing to the nearest wall.

slow **5** **Left foot** takes a step forwards, turning to the left.

quick **6** **Right foot** takes a step to the side, still turning to the left. By now you should have turned enough so that you are backing the nearest wall.

quick **7** **Left foot** takes a step backwards, still turning slightly to the left. On this step and on steps 8, 9, and 10 the dance pattern turns left so as to follow a curve – 90 degrees in all.

slow **8** **Right foot** takes a step backwards, still turning slightly to the left and guiding the lady by pressure on her back, with the heel and finger tips of your right hand, for her to take over the forwards momentum of the dance.

quick **9** **Left foot** takes a step backwards, still turning slightly left.

quick **10** **Right foot** takes a step backwards, completing the turn to the left and leaving you with your left shoulder pointing towards the nearest wall so you are backing the line of dance.

slow **11** **Left foot** takes a step backwards, starting to turn to the right.

slow **12** **Right foot** takes a small step to the side, drawing the foot along the floor into position. Remaining on flat feet, continue to turn strongly to finish 'facing diagonally to centre'.

slow **13** **Left foot** takes a step forwards.

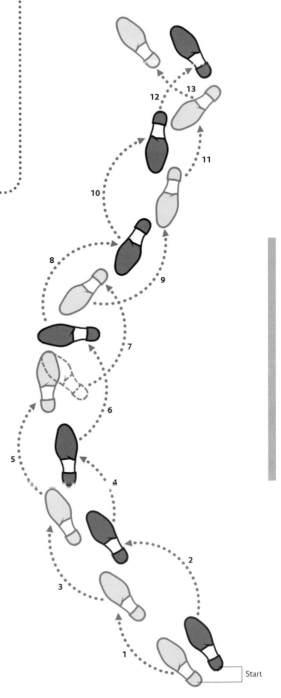

must know

Heel pull action
As both partners complete step 12, the foot without weight will close (brush) towards the foot with full weight before moving: man forwards, lady backwards, on step 13.

Walk and Curving Feather Step to Reverse Wave (continued)

count: **Lady's Steps**

Start with your left shoulder pointing towards the nearest wall and then turn 45 degrees to your left to finish 'backing diagonally to centre'.

slow **1 Right foot** takes a step backwards.

slow **2 Left foot** takes a step backwards, turning slightly to the right.

quick **3 Right foot** takes a step backwards, still turning to the right.

quick **4 Left foot** takes a step backwards, with partner stepping to your right of your feet ('partner outside').

slow **5 Right foot** takes a step backwards, turning to the left. This is the first step of a Heel Turn.

quick **6 Left foot** closes to right foot, still turning to the left to face diagonally to the nearest wall.

quick **7 Right foot** takes a step forwards, still turning slightly to the left. On this and steps 8, 9 and 10 the dance pattern follows a curve to the left turning 90 degrees.

slow **8 Left foot** takes a step forwards. Then your partner will indicate by pressure with his right hand that you should take some consecutive forwards steps. Ensure that you maintain good body contact and that you push the man backwards.

quick **9 Right foot** takes a step forwards, still turning slightly left.

quick **10 Left foot** takes a step forwards, completing the slight turn to the left, leaving you with your right shoulder pointing towards the nearest wall, 'facing the line of dance'.

slow **11 Right foot** takes a step forwards. starting to turn to the right.

slow **12 Left foot** takes a step to the side, still turning strongly to the right. You will now be 'backing diagonally to centre'.

slow **13 Right foot** takes a step backwards.

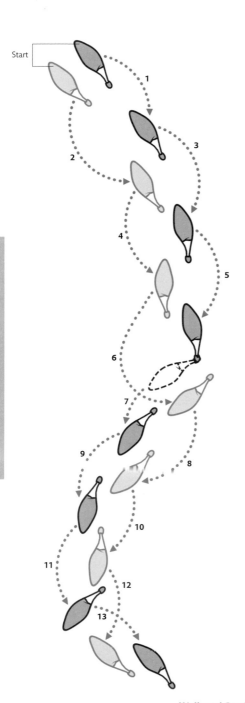

Start

1

2

3

4

5

6

7

8

9

10

11

12

13

must know

Heel turn
In this group, steps 5, 6 and 7 comprise the lady's heel turn. Because the lady continues turning while feet are together you might feel there is a discrepancy in respect of the direction the man and lady are facing. This is not so and when the dynamics are applied all will work out.

Walk and Curving Feather Step to Reverse Wave

1

count: slow

M **Left foot** takes a step forwards.

L **Right foot** takes a step backwards.

2

count: slow

M **Right foot** takes a step forwards, turning slightly to the right.

L **Left foot** takes a step backwards, turning slightly to the right.

5

count: slow

M **Left foot** takes a step forwards, turning to the left.

L **Right foot** takes a step backwards, turning to the left. This is the first step of a Heel Turn.

6

count: quick

M **Right foot** takes a step to the side, still turning to the left. You should have turned enough so that you are backing the nearest wall.

L **Left foot** closes to right foot, still turning to the left to face diagonally to the nearest wall.

3

count: quick

M Left foot takes a step forwards, still turning to the right.

L Right foot takes a step backwards, still turning to the right.

4

count: quick

M Right foot takes a step forwards, stepping to your left of your partner's feet ('outside partner'). By now you should have turned to be facing the line of dance.

L Left foot takes a step backwards, with partner stepping to your right of your feet ('partner outside').

7

count: quick

M Left foot takes a step backwards, still turning slightly to the left.

L Right foot takes a step forwards, still turning slightly to the left.

On this step and steps 8, 9 and 10 the dance pattern follows a curve to the left turning 90 degrees.

8

count: slow

M Right foot takes a step backwards, still turning slightly to the left and guiding the lady, by pressure on her back, to take over the forwards momentum.

L Left foot takes a step forwards. Partner will indicate that you should take some consecutive forwards steps.

(continued overleaf)

Walk and Curving Feather Step to Reverse Wave (continued)

9

count: quick

M   **Left foot** takes a step backwards, still turning slightly left.

L   **Right foot** takes a step forwards, still turning slightly left.

10

count: quick

M   **Right foot** takes a step backwards, completing the turn to the left, and with your left shoulder now pointing towards the nearest wall.

L   **Left foot** takes a step forwards, completing the turn to the left, and with your right shoulder now pointing towards the nearest wall.

12

count: slow

M   **Right foot** takes a small step to the side, drawing the foot along the floor. Remaining on flat feet, continue to turn strongly to finish 'facing diagonally to centre'.

L   **Left foot** takes a step to the side, still turning strongly to the right.

11

count: slow

M Left foot takes a step backwards, starting to turn to the right.

L Right foot takes a step forwards, starting to turn to the right.

13

count: slow

M Left foot takes a step forwards.

L Right foot takes a step backwards.

want to know more?

• If you're learning without a partner it's particularly advisable to join a dance school.

• To help find a dance studio, as well as local newspapers, look out for small ads in newsagents' and other shop windows. Notice boards in your local library are another source worth viewing.

• Buy the CD 'Take Your Partners Please – Slow Foxtrot', by the Ray Hamilton Orchestra.

• Widen your repertoire of dances; why not try Latin dance, see *Need to Know? Latin Dancing*.

weblinks

• For more information on the Slow Foxtrot visit: en.wikipedia.org/wiki /SlowFoxtrot

• For a wide range of dance services: www.dancematrix.com

• For websites of dance teachers' organizations, see pages 183-4 .

Glossary

Backing diagonally to centre: An indication of where the dancer is in relation to the movement of the dance around the room. Stand with the nearest wall on your left side and your body at right angles to it – to be 'backing diagonally to centre', turn 45 degrees to the left.

Backing diagonally to wall: An indication of where the dancer is in relation to the movement of the dance around the room. The 'wall' in the term is the one along which the dance will progress. Stand with the nearest wall on your left side and your body at right angles to it – to be 'backing diagonally to wall', turn 45 degrees to the right.

Backing line of dance: When the dancer is backing the imaginary line of dance (see Line of dance) then he or she is 'backing line of dance'.

Body sway: A tilt of the body to the left or the right from a vertical position. Body sway will be used naturally to lean slightly in towards the centre of rotation of turning dance figures.

Body swing: This refers to the momentum the body achieves when dancing freely and which helps create a smooth flowing dance.

Dance patterns: The various steps and figures used in dancing make patterns on the floor that are called 'dance patterns'.

Facing diagonally to centre: An indication of where the dancer is in relation to the movement of the dance round the room. Stand with the nearest wall on your right side and your body at right angles to it, then turn 45 degrees to the left to be 'facing diagonally to centre'.

Facing diagonally to wall: An indication of where the dancer is in relation to the movement of the dance round the room. Face the line of dance (see below), then turn 45 degrees to the right to be 'facing diagonally to wall'.

Facing line of dance: Face the imaginary line defined as the line of dance (see below).

Fall-away position: Standing in the promenade position, the man's left foot takes a step backwards and the lady's right foot takes a step backwards.

Fast syncopation: Syncopation is variance of the basic rhythm either by changing the emphasis or interloping additional beats or omitting beats. 'Fast syncopation' in dance is when a string of rapidly interpolated steps are inserted into the basic rhythmic pattern.

Figure: A series of steps linked together as a unit.

Foot remains in place: The foot remains in the position previously achieved and the weight of your body is retained on it.

4/4 Time: A musical term, sometimes called common time, to indicate that there are four crotchets, or beats, in each bar of music, as in the Social Foxtrot.

Leg swing: The free movement of the leg with the hip as fulcrum, from one position to another.

Line of dance: An imaginary line parallel with the wall along which the dance moves. It progresses in an anti-clockwise direction around the room, and in a rectangular room it turns 90 degrees at each corner.

Normal position: In each dance the man and the lady mostly hold one another in a manner peculiar to that dance. The hold for the majority of the dance is referred to as the 'normal position'. Variants will occur from time to time and will be defined as required.

Outside partner: A forwards step usually on the right foot to your left of your partner's feet. It may also be left foot forwards to your right of both your partner's feet.

Partner outside: A backwards step on either foot where your partner is stepping forwards 'outside partner' (see above).

Polka rhythms: Steps taken with a slight jumping action from ball of foot to ball of foot.

Promenade position: From the Close Hold, the man leads the lady to turn her right side away from him to form a V-shape. From the Open Hold, both the man and the lady turn outwards from each other – the man to the left and the lady to the right, forming a V shape.

Rhythm break, rightwards or leftwards: A sideways group of steps using the basic rhythm of the dance but not closing the feet neatly.

Skipping steps: Steps taken with a slight forwards jump on the supporting foot as the other foot moves to its next position.

3/4 Time: A musical term to indicate that are three crotchets, or beats, in each bar of music.

Need to know more?

Choosing a dance studio

How do you select an appropriate school? Your main concern should be to ensure that your teacher has one of the three major qualification levels in one of the recognized teachers' organizations.

Under the heading 'Teachers' Organizations' you will see listed eight different bodies. The membership of each of these consists of dance teachers who have passed the appropriate examinations of the organisation. They are all members of, and are overseen by, a loosely knit body known as the British Dance Council, and all conform to common standards. If you contact them they will let you know their members in your area.

There are three levels of qualification. In ascending order they are: Associate (A), Licentiate (L) – sometimes called Member (M) – and Fellow (F), the highest level. The name of the association or society is often abbreviated to initials.

In respect of the dances in this book, teachers can have qualified in either a ballroom branch (BB) or a Latin branch (LA) of the appropriate body and this will sometimes be added to the qualification. For example, Lyndon Wainwright FIDTA (BB & LA) and Lynda King FIDTA (BB & LA) – Fellow of the International Dance Teachers' Association (Ballroom and Latin Branches).

Finally, many people are put off joining a school of dance by feelings of inadequacy or embarrassment. It is a great mistake. Dance teachers do realise this and you will be made welcome and made to feel comfortable irrespective of your previous experience.

UK dance organizations

Ballroom Dancers' Federation
12 Warren Lodge Drive
Kingswood
SURREY KT20 6QN
Tel/Fax: 01737 833737

Ballroom Dancers' Federation International
PO Box 2075, Kenley
SURREY CR8 5YP
Tel/Fax: 020 8763 1368

British Dance Council
Terpsichore House
240 Merton Road
South Wimbledon
LONDON SW19 1EQ
Tel: 020 8545 0085
Fax: 020 8545 9225

Central Council of Physical Recreation
Francis House, Francis Street
LONDON SW1P 1DE
Tel: 020 7854 8500
Fax: 020 7854 8501
www.ccpr.org.uk

Council for Dance Education and Training
Toynbee Hall
28 Commercial Street
LONDON E1 6LS
Tel: 020 7247 4030
Fax: 020 7247 3404
www.cdet.org.uk

World dance organization

World Dance and Dance Sport Council
Karolinastrassa 20
28195 BREMEN
Germany
Tel: +49 421 13162
Fax: +49 421 14942

Teachers' organizations

Allied Dancing Association
137 Greenhill Road
LIVERPOOL L18 7HQ
Tel: 0151 724 1829

British Association of Teachers of Dancing
23 Marywood Square
GLASGOW G41 2BP
Tel: 0141 423 4029
www.batd.co.uk

Imperial Society of Teachers of Dancing
22–26 Paul Street
LONDON EC2A 4QE
Tel: 020 7377 1577
Fax: 020 7247 8979
www.istd.org

International Dance Teachers' Association
76 Bennett Road
BRIGHTON BN2 5JL
Tel: 01273 685652
Fax: 01273 674388
www.idta.co.uk

National Association of Teachers of Dancing
44–47 The Broadway
THATCHAM
Berkshire RG19 3HP
Tel: 01635 868888
Fax: 01635 872301
www.natd.org.uk

Northern Counties Dance Teachers' Association
67 Elizabeth Drive
Palmersville
NEWCASTLE-UPON-TYNE
Tyne & Wear NE12 9QP
Tel: 0191 268 1830

Scottish Dance Teachers' Alliance
101 Park Road
GLASGOW G4 9JE
Tel: 0141 339 8944
Fax: 0141 357 4994

United Kingdom Alliance
Centenary House
38-40 Station Road
BLACKPOOL
Lancs FY4 1EU
Tel: 01253 408828
Fax: 01253 408066

Dance studios

England

Bedfordshire
Dance Fantasia
15 The Magpies
Bushmead
LUTON LU2 7XT
Tel: 01582 488529

Rayners School of Dancing
The Hall
Ashwell Avenue
Sundon Park
LUTON LU3 3AU
Tel: 01582 592510

Berkshire
Blanche Bateman Studio of Ballroom Dancing
23 Buckingham Avenue East
SLOUGH SL1 3EB
Tel/Fax: 01753 520003

Spotlights Dance Centre
15 Marks Road
WOKINGHAM RG41 1NR
Tel: 0118 979 5044
www.spotlightsdance.com

Buckinghamshire
The Jill Foster Dance Centre
130 Wolverton Road
Stony Stratford
MILTON KEYNES MK11 1DN
Tel: 01908 563029

The Suzanne Lear School of Dancing
24 Sospel Court
FARNHAM ROYAL SL2 3BT
Tel: 01753 644612

Tracey's Dancezone
14 Cressey Avenue
Shenley Brook End
MILTON KEYNES MK5 7EL
Tel: 01908 504271

Cambridgeshire
Brown's Dance Studio
286 Lincoln Road
PETERBOROUGH PE3 9PJ
Tel: 01733 554282

DMJ Dancing
8 Othello Close
Hartford
HUNTINGDON PE29 1SU
Tel: 01480 458522/07803 184826

Maureen's School of Dancing
14 Augustus Way
CHATTERIS PE16 6DR
Tel: 01354 693218

Cheshire
Dance Fever
2 Ashfield House
Ashfield Road
SALE M33 7FE
Tel: 07973 921714
www.dancefever.uk.com

Lucy Diamond School of Dancing
Middlewich British Legion and Centura Club
MIDDLEWICH CW10 3AF
Tel: 07929 051917

J. J. Foulds School of Dancing
Ashpoole House
LOWTON WA3 1BG
Tel: 01942 671270

Northwich Dance Company
c/o 16 Mayfair Drive
Kingsmead
NORTHWICH CW9 8GF
Tel: 01606 49050

Village Dancentre
9 Park Road Hale
ALTRINCHAM WA15 9NL
(Classes in Bowdon, Hazel Grove and Offerton)
Tel: 0161 928 9705

Cornwall
Tyler School of Dancing
'Topspin'
32 Trenance Avenue
NEWQUAY TR7 2HQ
Tel: 01637 873789

Derbyshire
Samantha-Jane Loades Academy of Dance
36a Frederick Avenue
ILKESTON DE7 4DW
Tel: 0115 932 3560/07946 389497

Devon
Chance to Dance
65 Churchill Road
EXMOUTH EX8 4DT
Tel: 01395 269782

Dance Latino
Renmark House, 26 Elm Road
EXMOUTH EX8 2LG
Tel: 01395 277217

Lansdowne Dance Centre
16 Cadeell Park Road
TORQUAY TQ2 7JU
Tel: 01803 613580

Tanner-J Dance Zone
12 Redvers Grove
Plympton
PLYMOUTH PL7 1HU
Tel: 01752 283828

Westcountry Dance Studios
Inglenook Rockbeare Hill
EXETER EX5 2EZ
Tel: 01404 822942

Dorset

**Bridport School of Dancing
and Lyric Studios Stagecraft**
9 Barrack Street
BRIDPORT DT6 3L4
Tel: 01308 427769
Dance Majic
Newtown Liberal Hall
316 Ringwood Road
Parkstone
POOLE BH14 0RY
Tel: 01202 723381
www.dorsetdancecentre.co.uk

Durham

Lee Green Dance Centre
5 Lee Green
NEWTON AYCLIFFE DL5 5HN
Tel: 01325 318239
Richardson's Dance Studio
27–28 Fore Bondgate
BISHOP AUCKLAND DL14 7PE
Tel: 01388 609899
www.richardsonsdance
studio.co.uk

Essex

Anderson Dance Group
226 Perry Street
BILLERICAY CM12 0NZ
Tel: 01277 633509
www.andersondancegroup.
co.uk
A and M Dancing
5 St Mary's Road
BRAINTREE CM7 3JP
Tel: 01376 325753
Athene School of Dancing
Church Green
Broomfield
CHELMSFORD CM1 7BD
Tel: 0845 004 3062
www.pleisuredance.biz
King's Palais of Dance
WCA Market Road
WICKFORD SS12 0AG
Tel: 01375 375810
Spotlight DanceWorld
739a London Road
WESTCLIFF-ON-SEA SS0 9ST
Tel: 01702 474374

**Steps Ahead School of
Dancing**
10 Griffith Close
Chadwell Heath
ROMFORD RM8 1TW
Tel: 07739 314596
www.stepsaheaddancing.com
Western Dance Centre
38 High Street
HADLEIGH SS9 2PB
Tel: 01702 559836
www.westerndancecentre.co.uk

Gloucestershire

Dancestars
37 Parry Road
GLOUCESTER GL1 4RZ
Tel: 01452 423 234
**Foot Tappers School of
Dancing**
55 Dunster Close
TUFFLEY GL4 0TP
Tel: 01452 419324

Greater London

CK's Academy of Dance
16 St Marks Road
Bush Hill Park
ENFIELD EN1 1BE
Tel: 020 8482 4885
www.ckdance.co.uk
Dance Dayz
171 Henley Avenue
North Cheam
SUTTON SM3 9SD
Tel: 020 8641 5492
Dance Unlimited
74 Beresford Avenue
SURBITON KT5 9LW
Tel: 020 8339 8875
www.dance-unlimited.org
Hotsteps Dance Club
11b Station Road
ORPINGTON BR6 0RZ
Tel: 01689 822702
www.hotsteps.co.uk
Langley School of Dancing
Shepperton Village Hall
High Street
SHEPPERTON TW17 9AU
Tel: 020 8751 2177
www.langleydancing.co.uk

Pam's Dance Vogue
73 Hoylake Crescent
ICKENHAM UB10 8JQ
Tel: 01895 632143
Charles Richman
31 St Andrews Avenue
HORNCHURCH RM12 5DU
Tel: 07956 957038
Rita Sinclair
c/o 117 Burnway
HORNCHURCH RM11 3SW
Tel: 01708 471208/
07887 511468
**Wedding and Emergency
Dance Lessons**
The Dance Matrix – Nationwide
Head Office: 115 Crofton Way
ENFIELD EN2 8HR
www.dancematrix.com
**Wright Rhythm Dancing
School**
133 First Avenue
Bush Hill Park
ENFIELD EN1 1BP
Tel: 07801 414959
Yvonne's Dance School
12 Matlock Crescent
CHEAM SM3 9SP
www.dance-technique.co.uk

Hampshire

**Angela's School of
Dancing**
Queens Road
ALDERSHOT GU11 3JE
Tel: 01252 332239
Basingstoke Dance Centre
25 Cavalier Road
Old Basing
BASINGSTOKE RG24 0EW
Tel: 01256 461665
**Dance Connection of
Gosport**
Brune Park Community School
Military Road
GOSPORT PO12 3BJ
Tel: 01329 314061/
023 8046 6181
www.groups.msn.co.uk/
danceconnectionofgosport

Need to know more?

Diamond Dancentre
9 Queens Road
FARNBOROUGH GU14 6DJ
Tel: 01252 342118
www.diamonddancentre.
co.uk

**Diment Macdonald Dance
Centre**
10 Spring Crescent
Portswood
SOUTHAMPTON SO17 2GA
Tel: 023 8055 4192
www.dimentmacdonald.co.uk

Fiesta Dance School
Moose Centre
Churchill Way
BASINGSTOKE RG21 7QU
Tel: 07879 494911

Footsteps Dance School
73 Britten Road
Brighton Hill
BASINGSTOKE RG22 4HN
Tel: 01256 475619

Shuffles Dance Studio
Oak Farm Community
School
Chaucer Road
FARNBOROUGH
Tel: 01252 314291/
07774 151545
www.shuffles-dance.com

Spinners Dance Studio
4 Pardoe Close
Hedge End
SOUTHAMPTON SO30 0NE
Tel: 01489 781513

Herefordshire
**Allseasons School of
Dance and Leisure**
35 Friar Street
HEREFORD HR4 0AS
Tel:01432 353756
www.allseasonsdance.co.uk

**Maureen's School of
Dancing**
41 Greengage Rise
Melbourn
ROYSTON SG8 6DS
Tel: 01763 261680

Hertfordshire
Apton Dance Studio
Part Millers Two
The Maltings
BISHOPS STORTFORD
CM23 3DH
Tel: 01279 465381
www.aptondancestudio.com

The Dance Centre
1st Floor
24–26 High Street
HEMEL HEMPSTEAD HP1 3AE
Tel: 01442 252367

Kent
J. B.'s Dance Studio
90 St Michaels Street
FOLKESTONE CT20 1LS
Tel: 01303 252706

**Hurcombe School of
Dancing**
34 Oxen Lease
Singleton
ASHFORD TN23 4YT
Tel: 01233 643411

**Nicola Hyland School of
Dancing**
Sturry Social Centre
Sturry
NR. CANTERBURY
Tel: 07710 566827

**Page/Mason School of
Dancing**
7 St Peter's Court
BROADSTAIRS CT10 2UU
Tel: 01843 863730

Rose School of Dancing
8 Bearsted Close
GILLINGHAM ME8 6LS
Tel: 01634 360105/235878

Lancashire
Haslingden Dance Centre
IDL Club George Street
Haslingden
ROSSENDALE
Tel: 01706 228693

Liberal School of Dancing
114 Burnley Road
Broadclough
BACUP OL13 8DB
Tel: 01706 872556

Northern Dance Connection
12 Holly Close
Clayton Le Woods
CHORLEY PR6 7JN
Tel: 01772 314551
www.dancefreeman.com

Leicestershire
118 Dance Studio
118 Charles Street
LEICESTER LE1 1LB
Tel: 0116 251 7073/289 2518

Premier Dancing Ltd
29–31 New Bond Street
LEICESTER LE1 4RQ
Tel: 0116 269 3618/251 1084
www.premierdance.co.uk

Lincolnshire
Cliftons Dance Academy
3 Turnberry Approach
Waltham
GRIMSBY DN37 0UQ
Tel: 01472 822270

Go Dance Studios
Tamer Court
Church Lane
SLEAFORD NG34 7DE
Tel: 01529 300930

Stevenson School of Dancing
Above 513 Grimsby Road
CLEETHORPES DN35 8AN
Tel: 01472 601069

London
A.C.W. Dance Studio
Office only:
Garden Flat
20a Melrose Road
SOUTHFIELDS SW18 1NE
Tel: 020 8871 0890
www.acwdancestudio.com

Central London Dance
13 Blandford Street
W1U 3DF
Tel: 020 7224 6004

Dancewise
1st Floor
370 Footscray Road
NEW ELTHAM SE9 2AA
Tel: 020 8294 1576
www.dancewise.co.uk

Flynn School of Dancing
40 Jago Close
PLUMSTEAD SE18 2TY
Tel: 01322 381070

Footsteps Stage School
(Chingford Loughton and
Chigwell)
Tel: 020 8500 6943
www.footstepsdance
school.com

**Linda Fountain School
of Dancing**
6 Voss Court
STREATHAM SW16 3BS
Tel: 020 8679 3040

Dancemore
Robert Clack Centre
DAGENHAM RM8 1JU
Tel: 07761 209463

Bruce Smith Studio
Lacey Hall
Hazelwood Lane
PALMERS GREEN N13 6DE
Tel: 01920 468857/
07702 188368

Greater Manchester
A Touch of Class
139 High Street
BOLTON BL3 1LX
Tel: 01204 861242

Danceland
55 Bridgewater Street
Little Hulton
WORSLEY M38 9ND
Tel: 0161 703 9577

Granada School of Dancing
St.Matthews Road
(above Conservative Club)
Edgeley
STOCKPORT SK3 9AM
Tel: 0161 480 6588

Parkfield Dance Centre
56 Eastwood Road
NEW MOSTON M40 3TF
Tel: 0161 682 4172

Sandham's Dance Studio
9a Peel Street
Farnworth
BOLTON BL4 8AA
Tel: 01204 795130
www.sandhams.co.uk

Village Dancentre
9 Park Road Hale
ALTRINCHAM WA15 9NL
Tel: 0161 928 9705

Merseyside
Debonaires at the Regency
84 Prescot Road
ST HELENS WA10 3TY
Tel: 01744 759466
www.debonairesatthe
regency.com

**The New Regency Dance
Centre**
c/o 35 Hill School Road
ST HELENS WA10 3BH
Tel: 01744 21061

Silhouette Dance Club
29 Hillbray Avenue
ST HELENS WA11 7DL
Tel: 01744 20136
www.silhouette-dance
club.co.uk

Pat Thompson Dance Centre
110 Northway
Maghull
LIVERPOOL L31 1EF
Tel: 0151 526 1056/526 2010

Norfolk
Connaught Dance Centre
1 Laxton Close
ATTLEBOROUGH NR17 1QY
Tel: 01953 455500

**Miller Dance and Performing
Arts Centre**
Units 1–3 Ropemakers Row
NORWICH NR3 2DG
Tel: 01603 488249
www.millerdance.co.uk

**Tempo Schools of
Dancing**
55 Mallard Way
Bradwell
GREAT YARMOUTH NR31 8LX
Tel: 01493 665558

Northamptonshire
Margo's Dance Centre
204 Windmill Avenue
KETTERING NN15 7DG
Tel: 01536 312002

Tempo Dance Studio
Bath Road, Tailby House
KETTERING NN16 8NL
Tel: 01536 723656
www.tempodancestudio.co.uk

Nottinghamshire
Ann Culley School of Dance
26 Main Street
PAPPLEWICK NG15 8FD
Tel: 0115 963 3428/
07711 946335

The L.A. School of Dance
13 Cheddar Close
Rainworth
MANSFIELD NG21 0HX
Tel: 01623 796431/
07984 079568

**Ray Needham School of
Dance**
9 Douglas Crescent
CARLTON NG4 1AN
Tel: 0115 841 1779/
07973 939378
www.rayneedham.co.uk

Oxfordshire
Abingdon Dance Studios
59 Swinburne Road
ABINGDON OX14 2HF
Tel: 01235 520195
www.abingdondance.co.uk

Sarah Ayers School of Dance
20 Wytham View
Eynsham
OXFORD OX29 4LU
Tel: 01865 881208

Somerset
Davies School of Dance
12 The Hedges
St Georges
WESTON SUPER MARE
BS22 7SY
Tel: 01934 521338
www.davies-school-of-
dance.co.uk

Langport Dance Centre
Bonds Farm
WEARNE (nr Langport)
TA10 0QQ
Tel: 01458 250322

Need to know more?

Belinda Orford
Wayside Shepperdine Road
Oldbury Naite
BRISTOL BS35 1RJ
Tel: 01454 415346
PJ's Dance Academy
c/o 8 Meadow Drive
WESTON SUPER MARE
BS24 8BB
Tel: 01934 823948/
07855 827464

Staffordshire
Flair Dance Academy
60 Etchinghill Road
RUGELEY WS15 2LW
Tel: 01889 579558
Shaftesbury School of Dancing
48 Palmers Green
Hartshill
STOKE ON TRENT ST4 6AP
Tel: 01782 618180
www.shaftesburydance.com

Suffolk
Lait Dance Club
St Matthew's Hall
Clarkson Street
IPSWICH IP1 2JD
Tel: 01473 215543
www.laitdanceclub.co.uk

Sussex
Crawley Dance Academy
3 Tushmore Avenue
Northgate
CRAWLEY RH10 8LF
Tel: 01293 612538

Tyne & Wear
Newcastle Dance Centre
36–38 Grainger Park Road
NEWCASTLE-UPON-TYNE
NE4 8RY
Tel: 0191 273 9987
www.newcastledance
centre.co.uk

Warwickshire
DancinTime
Terpsichore Cottage
81 Alcester Road
STUDLEY B80 7NJ
Tel: 01527 852178
Jonstar School of Dancing
22 Gibson Crescent
BEDWORTH CV12 8RP
Tel: 024 7631 6592

West Midlands
Boscott's Dance Club
5 Long Wood
BOURNEVILLE B30 1HT
Tel: 0121 459 9167
Broadway Dance Centre
42 Livingstone Road
Perry Barr
BIRMINGHAM B20 3LL
Tel: 0121 356 4663
Inspire School of Dance
11 Alverley Road
Daimler Green
COVENTRY CV6 3LH
Tel: 024 7659 3359
Touch of Class Dancentre (incorporating The Midland Stage School of Performing Arts)
Holloway Hall
Court Passage, off Priory Street
DUDLEY DY1 3EX
Tel: 01384 235999/
07970 889251
www.freewebs.com/
touch-of-class-dancentre

Worcestershire
Catshill Dance Centre
Gibb Lane Catshill
BROMSGROVE B61 0JP
Tel: 01527 873638

Yorkshire East
Lacey School of Dancing
17 Grassdale Park
BROUGH HU15 1EB
Tel: 01482 666863
Lyndels Dancing Club
3 The Avenue
Melrose Street
HULL HU3 6EY
Tel: 01482 501248

Yorkshire North
Perry's Dancing
14 Haw Bank Court
SKIPTON BD23 1BY
Tel: 01756 794468 or 07900 285853
Playcraft Leisure School of Dancing
13 Kestrel Drive
Scotton
CATTERICK GARRISON DL9 3LX
Tel: 01748 830508

Yorkshire South
Joanne Armstrong School of Dancing
14 North End Drive
Harlington
DONCASTER DN5 7JS
Tel: 07979 758696
www.joannearmstrong.co.uk
Dentonia School of Dancing
Barnsley Road
Wombwell
BARNSLEY S73 8DJ
Tel: 01226 754684
Drapers Dance Centre
High Street
Beighton
SHEFFIELD S20 1ED
Tel: 0114 269 5703
Helen Neill School of Dance
41 Barnsley Road
Penistone
SHEFFIELD S36 8AD
Tel: 07771 610868

Yorkshire West

The D. M. Academy
The Studios
Briggate
SHIPLEY BD17 7BT
Tel: 01274 585317
www.dmacademy.co.uk

Horsforth Dance Academy
44 Hawksworth Avenue
GUISELEY
LEEDS LS20 8EJ
Tel: 01943 875894

Darren Peters Dance Centre
(Schools in Halifax, Thornton
and Wilsden)
Tel: 07879 447106

Shandaw School of Dance
Serendipity Cottages
107–109 Gilstead Lane
Gilstead
BINGLEY BD16 3LH
Tel: 01274 510612
www.shandaw.co.uk

**Wakefield Dance Group/
Wakefield City Slickers**
82 Walton Lane
Sandal
WAKEFIELD WF2 6HQ
Tel: 01924 256624
www.members.lycos.co.uk/
davidherries/index.htm

The Windsor School of Dancing
5 Willow Street
Girlington
BRADFORD BD8 9LT
Tel: 01274 488961
www.windsorballroom.co.uk

York Dance Studios
8 Radcliffe Road
Milnsbridge
HUDDERSFIELD HD3 4LX
Tel: 01484 643120
www.yorkdance.co.uk

Scotland

Johnny & Eleanor Banks
13 Paisley Avenue
EDINBURGH EH8 7LB
Tel: 0131 6613447

Ms N. Clark
61 Balnagowan Drive
GLENROTHES
Fife KY6 2SJ
Tel: 01592 772685

John & Charlotte Comrie
76 Balmoral Avenue
Balmoral Gardens
Glenmavis
AIDRIE ML6 0PY

Andrew Cowan School of Dance
Community Central Hall
304 Maryhill Road
GLASGOW G20 7YE
Tel: 0141 6342129

Dees Dancing
PO Box 5456
GLASGOW G77 5LN
Tel: 0141 639 8300
www.deesdancing.co.uk

David Johnston
47 Polmont Road
Lauriestone
FALKIRK FK2 9QS
Tel: 01324 623007

Star Ballroom
10 Burnside Street
DUNDEE
Tel: 01382 611388

Christine Stevenson
(Various venues)
24 Ashgillhead Road
Larkhall
MOTHERWELL ML9 3AS
Tel: 01698 887296

Diane Swan Ballroom Dance Studio
72 Balnagask Road
ABERDEEN, AB11 8RE
Tel: 01224 876444

Warrens
(Various Glasgow venues)
Tel: 0141 942 7670

Wales

Dance Kingdom
Pharaoh House
Station Yard
New Dock Road
LLANELLI SA15 2EF
Tel: 01554 771543
dancekingdom.co.uk

Edwards Studio of Dance
Victoria House
Andrews Road
Llandaff North
CARDIFF CF14 2JP
Tel: 01222 575487 or
01222 843120

New Cottage Dance Centre
Ystrad-Mynach
HENGOED CF82 7ED
Tel: 01443 815909

Richards School of Dance
144 Rhys Street
Trealaw
TONYPANDY CF40 2QF
Tel: 07929 079403

Index

Acknowledgements

Thanks to Mr B. Perry of Dancemore and Mr M. Kyberd of Michael's Dance Studio for providing the locations for the dance photography, and to the dancers:

Social Foxtrot: Keiran Smith and Kelly Neville
Waltz: Lee Delf and Kelly Dall
Quickstep: Brenda and Clive Phillips
Rock 'n' Roll and Jive: Carl Webb and Emma Lee

Tango: Katrina Eastabrook and Darren Coman
Slow Foxtrot: Kyle Magee and Theodora Karavasili

Photo credits
Bananastock Ltd. pp. 2, 8, 13 (right), 18, 78, 148, 151
Corbis pp. 128 (Royalty-free), 130 (Swim Ink 2, LLC)
Getty Images pp. 11, 50, 53, 81, 102, 105
Ron Self p. 6
All other photographs by Christopher H. D. Davis

Collins need to know?

Look out for these recent titles in Collins' practical and accessible need to know? series.

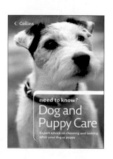

Other titles in the series:

To order any of these titles, please telephone 0870 787 1732 quoting reference 263H. For further information about all Collins books, visit our website: www.collins.co.uk